# THE SECRET PLACES
# OF DONEGAL

BOOK BY THE SAME AUTHOR

*Travel*
THE SECRET PLACES OF THE BURREN
THE WIND THAT ROUND THE FASTNET SWEEPS
THE MAGIC OF THE KERRY COAST
THE MAGIC OF THE SHANNON

*Biography*
TOMORROW TO BE BRAVE
AN IRISH PUBLISHER AND HIS WORLD
BOBBY SANDS AND THE TRAGEDY OF NORTHERN IRELAND

*Politics*
THE SHOOTING OF MICHAEL COLLINS
OPERATION BROGUE
THE STATESMAN

# THE SECRET PLACES OF DONEGAL

### JOHN M. FEEHAN

*We see things not as they are but as we are.*

KANT

ROYAL CARBERY BOOKS

Royal Carbery Books Limited, Cork
An Imprint of Mercier Press

© John M. Feehan, 1988

ISBN 978 1 78117 916 1

Transferred to Digital Print-on-Demand in 2024

# CONTENTS

| | |
|---|---|
| INTRODUCTION | 9 |
| ONE | 13 |
| *Bundoran – Glencolumbkille* | |
| TWO | 40 |
| *Glencolumbkille – Annagry* | |
| THREE | 66 |
| *Gweedore – Gartan* | |
| FOUR | 90 |
| *Gartan – Fanad – Dromboe* | |
| FIVE | 113 |
| *Inishowen – Aileach* | |
| A READING LIST | 139 |

DEDICATED
TO
LEONORE

# INTRODUCTION

*Man struggles to find life outside himself unaware that the life he is seeking is within him.*

KAHLIL GIBRAN

This book is different from other travel books in so far as it is not just an account of the physical beauties of Donegal but it is also a spiritual and intellectual exploration of one human being's reactions to its magnificent countenance. I sought a response from this beautiful county of mountains, lakes, valleys and deep fiords and I was rewarded by a wealth of answers. I allowed what I saw, whom I met and what happened to me to set the wheels of my mind turning and what I have written here is the partial result. It is as much a ramble through the mountains and valleys and seas of life as it is a ramble through Donegal. This captivating county is a superb setting for those chance discoveries which arouse emotions of anger and fun, of turmoil and peace. Each place I visited gave me a little of its own vibrant sparkling personality.

The attachment to visible and external things can be quite deadly. These attachments can overwhelm us and smother those thoughts of inspiration that come to us when we look inwards in silence so it is better to listen to the voice of the soul. I have tried to make the words of Tennyson my inspiration:

> Moreover something is or seems
> That touches me with mystic gleams
> Like glimpses of forgotten dreams –
> Of something felt, like something here;
> Of something done, I know not where
> Such as no language may declare.

Alas not all of what I have written is so edifying, but then life itself is far from edifying. Sadly a lot of places in Donegal evoke emotions of a very painful and unedifying kind. For most of its history it was a veritable death camp and the torture and brutality have left their scars.

One day I was discussing the Nazi atrocities in Holland with a Dutch businessman and he remarked: 'We cannot go on hating for ever.' Nevertheless he added a profound and wise statement: 'To forgive and forget is a counsel of perfection,' he said, 'one should forgive but one should never forget, especially in matters of politics and history. Evil tends to repeat itself if ignored.'

This advice has encouraged me to write much in this book which is sad, but I have tried to do so without rancour. It would be wrong to go on hating our enemies eternally but one should take prudent cognisance of what happened, since much of it is being repeated today.

Just as one should not blame the German people for the atrocities of the Nazis, neither should one blame the British people for the atrocities of the British Establishment. My experience is that a very skilful censorship has kept the knowledge of these atrocities from them. That seems to be the reason why British tourists, when they come on holiday to Ireland, buy thousands of Irish books on the Northern problem. They are simply unable to get them at home.

Misty

If, on the other hand, I seem to be a little facetious at times, then do not censure me too much. The devil loves gloomy people. If nature did not make us a little lighthearted then we might easily bring our lives to an end. On holiday it is very important to laugh, and sometimes to take a chance by letting ourselves get into a stupid situation. Darwin defined a fool as a man who never made an experiment. The secret of enjoyment however is not to laugh *at* people, but to laugh *with* them, and above all to laugh at oneself.

Don't let all those things I wrote about death upset you too much. I'll let you into another great secret. If you can

## INTRODUCTION

laugh at death it can hold no terrors for you. I think it was Rachael Field who said: 'The truth is ongoing. It is better to be left with a question than to be given an answer.'

There is no real sequence of travel you can follow in searching out the secret places of Donegal. They are everywhere and you can begin anywhere.

Most of the journeys described in this book were made in the summer of 1987, with a little cairn terrier, Misty, as my companion, and I would like to thank very sincerely those who helped me. The Donegal, Leitrim and Sligo Tourism Organisation gave me much useful assistance, especially Brigid Kerr of the Letterkenny office who went out of her way to provide me with valuable historical material. Others to whom I am indebted are: Eily Kilgannon, Lucius Emerson, Carole Devaney, Cathleen Cullen and Bernie Power. A special word of thanks to Hilary Richardson for her lovely illustrations. These kind people are, of course, in no way responsible for the opinions I express in this book.

Go mba fada buan iad go léir.

J.M.F.
Christmas 1987

ONE

# BUNDORAN – GLENCOLUMBKILLE

*Captains and conquerers leave a little dust*
*And kings a dubious legend of their reign.*
*The swords of Caesar, they are less*
   *than rust*
*The poet doth remain.*

SIR WILLIAM WATSON

I first got to know Donegal in the year of Our Lord – well, never mind – it was a long, long time ago anyway. I was eighteen, a student at University College, Galway and a volunteer member of a type of officers' training corps attached to the army and known by the name of the Regiment of Pearse. It was a great time to be alive and young. The then idealistic De Valera was in power and he was dismantling step-by-step the last chains which bound us to the British empire. Young Ireland was infected by his vision. There were no yuppies around then. Instead there was a kind of patriotic euphoria in the air and large numbers of students gave practical expression to this by speaking the Irish language whenever possible and by joining the armed forces in a unit dedicated to the memory of Pearse.

Each summer we went to Finner Camp, just outside Bundoran in County Donegal, for two weeks' training. These glorious weeks were a time of intense military activity coupled with daily swimming and bathing on the long, sunswept, sandy beaches. Night-time brought us to one of the many halls in Bundoran to dance with a dazzling selection of attractive Scottish girls who traditionally holidayed in this renowned resort.

It was in one of these halls that the lightning of Donegal struck. I fell in love. She was everything I had dreamed of – tall, slim, graceful, golden hair and a full firm bosom. When she smiled her snow-white teeth flashed like pearls. Her blue, entrancing eyes sparkled with joy. She danced with life and vitality when jiving and with grace and dignity when waltzing. When I gently eased her body closer to mine in one of those slow, sensual tangos fashionable at the time, she responded with modesty and coyness. She was eighteen and Scottish. Her name was Lily. I had idealised her so much that I was ever so slightly taken aback when she told me she worked in a ladies underwear factory. When I tried to draw her out a little further on the nature and variety of her work she quietly but fimly told me that we did not know each other well enough to discuss such matters. Nevertheless there was a hint in her voice that when we were better acquainted this subject could be referred to again.

Arm in arm we linked home to her lodgings. Summer had laid siege to the little town. It was the kind of night that filled the imagination with strange thoughts and mysterious inexplicable longings. With beguiling coquetry she confided in me that her mother would like her to marry a butcher in Glasgow who owned a nice terraced house with a back yard. Her mother warned her, too, to keep away from soldiers. Nevertheless before we said 'goodnight' she promised to meet me the following evening near a romantic little spot called the Fairy Bridge. We would not go dancing. Instead we would stroll along the sandhills by the edge of the sea listening to the lapping of the waves and the soft gentle sounds of twilight. Before we parted she gave me one of those rapturous kisses which spoke of the eternal.

I walked back the short distance to Finner Camp as if I were tripping on air. The warm breeze caressed my face and seemed to envelope my heart. The touch of love had awakened infinity in my soul and I was filled with vague undefined hopes. How innocent I was then! The madness of my young blood had not so far led me into foolish amorous adventures. I was naive, raw and guileless – but it was beautiful. Donegal was my Garden of Eden and I had just met Eve. I had yet a long way to go before I learned the wisdom of Montaigne's remark that most of life's pleasures caress and embrace us only to strangle us.

The next day in Finner we were on shooting practice but I was in such a turmoil that I could not even hit the target let alone score a bull's eye. I was so bad that the officer in charge told me I was only wasting good ammunition and he angrily marked my card 'put back for further instruction.' I could only think of Lily and the glorious evening ahead.

Later, in my tent I dressed myself up in a brown creased suit, cream shirt and put plenty of perfumed brilliantine on my hair. My tent-mate, who had helped me decorate myself, remarked that I was the nearest thing he saw to a model in a Grafton Street window.

'I will go with you as far as the gate of the camp,' he said, 'and give you a good send off.' I somehow felt he did not take the whole thing as seriously as I did, and for that I pitied him. We walked a hundred yards or so towards the main gate of the camp which was guarded by sentries. As we came near that gate he stopped and seemed as if he wanted to say something, then reeled and fell to the ground. I rushed to his side and knelt down to help him. His eyes rolled in his head, a reddish blue colour came to his face which was becoming horribly contorted. I shouted at one of the sentries to get a doctor quickly. By now a few others had gathered around. Someone opened the neck of his tunic, another put a coat under his head, yet another rubbed his hands and face vigorously, but nothing seemed to help. His complexion was becoming more and more blue and his eyes stared rigidly upwards. The army doctor arrived almost immediately. He felt his pulse, bent down and listened to his heart. After a moment or two he shook his head ominously and pronounced him dead. Then two medical orderlies arrived, lifted him on to a stretcher and brought him to the medical hut. I never saw him again.

The group dispersed and I was left standing alone. It was all over in five or six minutes. The life of a young man in the full bloom of his health and vigour was suddenly and savagely extinguished. I walked along towards Bundoran dazed and bewildered. It was as if a kind of stupor was paralysing me. I felt as if the sombre silence of another world had enveloped the evening and all life, including mine, was coming to an end.

When I got to Bundoran I was unable to face Lily. I realised that my burning love had become atrophied and I simply could not even think of anything so unsacred as going on a date with a girl. Instead I unkindly left poor Lily waiting and went into the church where I spent almost an hour in terrorised prayer.

I thought I too was going to die and hell was opening up in front of me. Presently an old, grey-haired priest in his seventies appeared and entered the confession box.

## BUNDORAN – GLENCOLUMCILLE

What better could I do than make my peace with God so that if I did die suddenly I would be prepared? When my turn came to go into the box I was still mighty confused and I found it difficult to formulate any sin. Then I thought of Lily and I confessed that I was guilty of having impure thoughts.

'What! What! What!' barked the old priest, 'Impure thoughts, impure thoughts. Very serious! Very serious!' He seemed to repeat everything a few times. He had a shake in his head and gave the impression that he was throwing the words from him. 'Did you take pleasure in them?' he asked. 'No father,' I answered. It did not seem to occur to either of us that it would be a trifle difficult to entertain bad thoughts without taking some pleasure in them. 'Ah well in that case it's not so bad, not so bad. All the same be careful of bad thoughts, bad thoughts. A great cure for bad thoughts is sport, sport, sport. Handball is very good, very good. If ever the devil tempts you again a game of handball will drive him away. For your penance say the Rosary, the Rosary.'

I was not sure whether he meant me to say one Rosary or two. However I said one in the church and for good measure I said another one on the way back to the camp.

This was how I came to know Donegal for the first time and it can never be said that it lacked drama.

Almost half a century later when I was writing this book, I was back in Bundoran. I could not find the dance-hall but I found a disco with flashing lights and screaming voices. Only the tomahawks and feathers were missing. As I listened I remembered a quip from the film *Jubilee:* 'We keep the music loud so that we can't hear the world falling apart.' I made my way to the church and said a silent prayer for my young companion who was so long dead and now almost completely forgotten.

As I prayed I remembered the unique cure the old priest with the shake gave me for impure thoughts. I do not know how effective it would be because any time during my life when I might have used it, there was, unfortunately, no ball-alley convenient. I left the church and strolled around the streets of Bundoran like Oisín searching for the Fianna. So very, very little had changed. On the strand the crowds were enjoying themselves in the summer sunshine. I drove out to the Fairy Bridge of our broken tryst and sat on the old wishing chair beside it. My heart was full of fondness for the beautiful young girl I had let down so long ago. I wondered where she was or what happened to her:

Dearest Lily, if your eyes ever catch these lines I hope that, even at this late hour, you will forgive me. A few days after our date, when I had balanced up a little, I did really try to find you. I called at your lodgings but the landlady told me you had gone home. She refused to give me your address because, as she said, she kept a respectable boarding house and no guest of hers would want any communication from a soldier. I do sincerely hope that you made it with the butcher and that you both had lots of children to gambol and frolic in the back yard of your terraced house. Please believe me, it wasn't that I didn't love you. It was just that, as so often happens with men, my cowardice smothered it. If you are still living I wish you all the joy and happiness that a graceful old age can bring. If you are dead I know that your home is amongst the angels.

A few miles out the Ballyshannon road I stopped the car and walked up a little hedge-rowed lane amid the perfume of wild flowers to an old world graveyard which holds the ruins of what was once a great monastic centre and place of worship, Finner Church. In the deathly silence I found myself slowly slipping backwards in time, slowly letting the imagination free. It was here the great St Columcille is said to have come when, having caused the deaths of more than three thousand men in battle, he was torn apart with anguish and remorse. What was he going to do with his life? How was he going to make amends? His close friend and adviser, St Molaisse, was superior and together they prayed, meditated and discussed tirelessly. The outcome was that Columcille, in the peace and quiet of this monastery, and with the counsel of his friend, made a vow to win back for Christianity as many souls as were killed in battle. From this decision was born the dream that was to end in far away Iona if this story is true. Here was where it all started fourteen hundred years ago – although many say that Finner Church is much later than Columcille's time.

Pensively I wandered around the old graveyard with only the dead for my companions. Misty frolicked and played, chasing butterflies and putting the headstones to a use for which they were never intended. All around me the terrible neglect expressed itself in weeds, nettles and briars. The words 'Gone but not forgotten' seemed strangely unreal. Yet there was one curious exception. The graves of eight or ten British soldiers buried here were clean, trimmed and well kept, as if cared for by some loving hand. Is there a lesson to be learned?

Finner military camp, where I did my training so many, many years ago, is a little further along this road. Today it is entirely changed and but a phantom of the past, a memory lost in the mists of politics. It now resembles a fortress with helicopters, armoured cars and other paraphernalia of war. The reason for this is that it has become primarily a base for border protection duties. 'Border protection duties' when translated simply means helping and assisting the British to maintain and copper-fasten their occupation of the six counties. Can one imagine the West German government having such a base on their eastern border to assist the KGB occupy East Germany? Or the Spanish government to keep the British in Gibraltar? Will we never learn? Will we never grow up? Must we always allow the British to fool and exploit us. It is hard for me especially, to accept that the army founded by Michael Collins and inspired by Pádraig Pearse is in danger of becoming the hind tit, the 'downstairs' part, of one of the cruellest and most criminal security forces in Europe. It is when I pass such places as Finner Camp that a sense of deep shame overwhelms me and I cannot help feeling that the leaders of our country might find some better use for our young men than helping the British.

This sense of shame in others may well be one of the principal reasons why morale in the army was hardly ever, at any time in its history, as low as it is today. The number of resignations among the officer class has recently reached concerned proportions. But could this be a good sign? Could it show that a substantial body of highly intelligent and dedicated men are no longer prepared to genuflect to the British ministry of defence? If this is so then it would be no more than an expression of the genuine army tradition, which was always Irish to the core.

At Ballyshannon I called into the White Horse Bar for a pint and a sandwich. Here I was welcomed by the beautiful and gracious Patricia Sweeny who gave me a copy of a most useful little booklet *A Walk around Ballyshannon* which was a great help to me in my ramble through the town.

This picturesque little town was built around the site of an ancient royal palace known as the Hill of Mullaghnashee, and is supposed to have been built by the Milesians thousands of years before Christ and that is why the Ballyshannon people claim that they are descended from the earliest people to come to Ireland.

I rambled around with Misty on the lead and took a look first at the old military barracks. I was hoping to catch a glimpse of a beautiful lady who haunts the barracks in the nude, much to the delight of the youth and the anger of their elders. She is known as the Green Lady, because they say she wears a green bra every St Patrick's Day. She is said to have been the wife of an officer 'caught in the act' by an enraged husband who ran her through with his sword. It seems as if the offending Romeo made a hasty escape unharmed. My luck however was out — not a sight of her to be seen anywhere.

I quite fail to understand the bad manners of an elderly carpenter who was doing some repairs there in the early years of the century. She appeared naked to him at the end of a large room. He just looked at her and continued working. She moved up to the centre of the room and he still ignored her. She glided up to within a foot or two of him and stood straight before him in all her nakedness, whereupon the old carpenter looked up at her and said: 'What the hell is wrong with you, missus, did you never see a carpenter before?' At that the poor lady vanished wondering if the age of chivalry had disappeared from Ballyshannon.

I strolled up the hill to St Anne's Church which is the last resting place of William Allingham (1824-1889), the poet of Ballyshannon. Allingham was not, of course, an Irish poet in the sense that Yeats, Synge, Ledwidge and many others were. Although he was brought up here it was in an Anglo-Irish milieu, a milieu whose homage, loyalty and devotion were given to the British crown and whose spiritual home was London.

All great writers give expression in one way or another to the people amongst whom they live, and in this way they become the voice of those who cannot easily speak for themselves. The Ballyshannon of Allingham's time was the home of a crushed and broken people. Thousands of starving men, women and children wandered the streets searching the ashpits and sewers for a crust of bread. Thousands more died of hunger and famine. One little child who stole two biscuits for her dying mother was caught and sentenced to six months in jail. Nobody spoke for those unfortunates; nor did anybody give expression to their cries and wild lamentations. Allingham lived among these poor suffering people but apart from one long poem 'Laurence Bloomfield' their sorrows seem to have passed him by. Daniel Corkery says if one is reared on alien porridge one does not take kindly to native grain. Allingham was reared on an alien Anglo-Irish porridge. He left his people without a voice and fritted away his life in the drawing-rooms of the London literati.

That was a great pity because he was a worthwhile poet and, unlike so many others, bore no ill-will towards the land of his birth. The selections of his poetry which usually appear in anthologies have served him badly. They are insipid and trashy. He was a great admirer of Keats and once when he visited the spot where Keats wrote *Ode to a Nightingale* he wrote what I think is one of his greatest poems – a poem which rarely finds its way into anthologies:

> A Nightingale upon a time
>   Here tried his tone
> Here too a poet made a rhyme
>   Bird, poet, are gone.

> Trivial at best the bird's gay song
> A shapeless trill
> The poet's rhyme will last as long
> As Hampstead Hill.

One of the really secret places of Donegal is here in Ballyshannon. It is a little cave called Catsby, just off the road to the Abbey of Assaroe. Above the entrance there is an unusual carved cross of unknown age. Inside there is a rugged stone altar and two bulláns. This was the hidden spot where the people of Ballyshannon came by stealth to hear Mass during the terrible penal days.

Having broken the Treaty of Limerick the British occupation forces in Ireland introduced savage pieces of legislation, which came to be known as the Penal Laws – the object of these laws was to make the Irish as British as the British themselves so that the country could be occupied and ruled with the least amount of trouble. The idea was that by smashing the Catholic religion and forcing Protestantism on the Irish the people would ultimately accept British rule. The destruction of Catholicism had little to do with religious beliefs. It was merely a political ploy in the furtherance of a policy of conquest, like the Nazi final solution for the Jews. Indeed I was told by Germans that the Nazis had translations made of relevant portions of the Penal Laws and that these formed the basis of some of their most repressive racial legislation.

Here in Catsby the people of Ballyshannon came to hear Mass on Sundays. During the Mass they had look-outs covering all approaches to keep watch for the British priest hunters. These bounty hunters were paid £20 for the capture of a priest and £10 for a layman, in our money £2,000 and £1,000 respectively. A captured priest was usually hanged without trial and a lay person sold into slavery in the West Indies.

Time and again the priest hunters made a swoop on Catsby but found nothing. The look-out system worked well. On one occasion a small group were unable to get away fast enough but they had the presence of mind to sit around the altar with a bottle of poteen and a deck of cards and were carousing to their hearts' content when the priest hunters arrived.

Nevertheless they were sometimes caught and Ballyshannon witnessed heart-rending scenes when fathers of families were torn from their wives and children who never saw them again.

Bishops too had to employ extraordinary ruses to minister to the people. Bishop McGonigal from Killybegs went around in the guise of a fisherman selling herrings and mackerel. Bishop Andrew Campbell of Kilmore travelled to fairs playing the bagpipes. There is a lovely portrait of him, in kilts with his bagpipes, hanging in the diocesan college in Cavan. St Oliver Plunkett dressed up as a British nobleman and went around on horseback visiting pubs and saloons. When some clerical busybody reported his conduct to Rome he replied to the Pope: 'I would have Your Holiness know that in order to perform my episcopal duties and minister to my diocese I find it necessary sometimes to carouse in the taverns and kiss the girls.' When I see a portrait of the sour face of Oliver I find it hard to imagine anyone wanting to kiss him.

Here in the shadow of the Assaroe ruins in the dark abandoned cavern of Catsby I could not help feeling proud of this noble ragged people who again and again were clubbed into insensibility but who never yielded, never gave up. Catsby had the effect of making me wish I could bring some of their great courage into my own life.

## BUNDORAN – GLENCOLUMCILLE

Northwards of Ballyshannon is Donegal town which is at least 2,000 years old and that makes it one of the oldest in Ireland. So when you stroll around its streets it is as if you were in Rome or Athens, moving through millenniums of history and culture and, like the cities of the ancient world, it too was destroyed by barbarians from the east.

In 1608 the British sacked it and burned its priceless library of manuscripts. Luckily, however, some of the monks escaped, brought their notes with them, and from these notes compiled the world famous *Annals of the Four Masters*. They were Michael and Peregrine Ó Clery, Peregrine Ó Duignean and Fearfeasa Ó Maolconry. Today they are commemorated by the Church of the Four Masters, built in 1935 and by an imposing obelisk in the centre of the town.

Not far from this centre are the ruins of Donegal castle, which was the home of the O'Donnell family – the best known of whom was the last Red Hugh. After the disastrous defeat at Kinsale and the equally disastrous flight of the earls the castle was confiscated and given as a gift to Sir Basil Brooke – a name which evokes much hatred among Irish Nationalists. Brooke extended the old castle in Jacobean style so that only a small portion of the original remains. Whenever I touch these hallowed stones I can conjure up a whole world of the past with a special focus on those months preceding the Battle of Kinsale in 1601.

Red Hugh O'Donnell and his colleague Hugh O'Neill believed that they could never drive the British out of Ireland without help from abroad. Militarily speaking I would disagree with that assessment, but then I wasn't around to advise them! They sought this help from England's enemy, King Philip of Spain, who was quick to see the advantages of helping the Irish. A united and friendly Ireland would give him an excellent base from which to commence operations against England, and ultimately invade, so he prepared and dispatched an expeditionary force which landed at Kinsale. The decision to land at Kinsale, 250 miles from Donegal, was the very height of stupidity, caused, in fact, by the interference of the Archbishop of Dublin. Anyone with an ounce of wit would have continued on and landed somewhere near Donegal where the united force of two armies, Irish and Spanish, would have been strong enough to route the British out of the country. The British surrounded the Spaniards at Kinsale. O'Neill and O'Donnell could not leave them without help since they had only six weeks supply of food, so in the depth of winter they marched their armies the 250 miles to Kinsale. O'Donnell's march is now reckoned one the greatest marches in history. Indeed the British commander Carew described it as 'the greatest march that has ever been heard of'. At Kinsale the Irish surrounded the British and here again another stupendous blunder was made. The English could have been starved into surrender in a few weeks. All the Irish had to do was wait. Instead they decided to attack. The plan to attack was betrayed so the English were waiting. In the skirmish that followed the Irish lost one thousand men and the English only six. Now the great question is why did the Irish not pull themselves together, regroup their forces and continue the siege. To this there is no satisfactory answer. They marched home to Donegal their morale broken. Seán O'Faolain shrewdly remarked: 'Mountjoy did not win the battle of Kinsale. O'Neill lost it.'

Here amid these old ruins we have a living link with those tragic days. The stones that we look at today are the same stones that heard the conferences and discussions of the military commanders, their hopes and expectations, all of which ended in naught except the enslavement of the Irish people for three hundred years. The whole destiny of Ireland for those three hundred years was decided within these walls. So step up to them, touch them, and say a silent prayer for the brave men who blundered so badly in those far off days.

Just outside Donegal town on the Killybegs road there is a right turning marked 'Lough Easke'. This short trip of fifteen miles around the lake is well worth while, especially in June when the rhododendrons are in bloom. Lough Easke is a place for lovers, or honeymoon couples whose vistas are still undimmed by the realities of living. Almost at every turn one meets scenery of unearthly beauty and little secret places where one can rest, relax and experience an awakening of the soul to boundless joy.

Back on the Killybegs road again the drive through the Glen of the Woods to Mountcharles is a sheer delight. Mountcharles should really be called by its old Irish name Tarelton, which means the 'meadow' or 'low land'.

Just beyond Mountcharles I took a road to the right signposted 'The Frosses' to visit the graveyard of this little village where rest the mortal remains of one of my favourite Irish poets, Ethna Carbery. Her grave is just inside the cemetery gate – adorned by a beautiful celtic cross inscribed both in Irish and English.

Ethna Carbery was born in Belfast but when she married the writer Seamus MacManus she moved to the Frosses. She was one of that band of talented women writers like Lady Gregory, Eva Gore-Booth and Alice Milligan who were the feminist expression of the great Irish literary renaissance pioneered by Yeats, Synge and many others. Just as she was on the verge of a promising career as a poet and after only a short idyllic marriage, she died. Her poetry was inspired by a deep love of Ireland, its oppressed poor as well as its heroes, and unlike Allingham, it gave voice to that strong violent Nationalism seething beneath the surface of the Irish people awaiting someone to give it expression:

> It was the soul of Ireland
> Awaking in speech she knew
> When the clans held the glens and the mountains
> And the hearts of her chiefs were true:
> She had stirred at last in her sleeping,
> She is folding her dreams away
> The hour of her destiny neareth
> And it may be today – today.

Some years after her death, in 1916, it was to burst into flames.

According to contemporary accounts she was a woman of great loveliness, kindness and talent who hoped through her writings to raise Ireland's drooping head and to sing away Ireland's sorrow.

As I stood there by her grave I found myself speaking to her across the years the beautiful words of Eva Gore-Booth:

> You whom I never knew
> Who lived remote, afar,
> Yet died the grief that tore my heart,
> Shall we live through the ages alone, apart,
> Or meet where the souls of the sorrowful are
> Telling the tale on some secret star,
> How your death from the root of my sorrow grew.
> You whom I never knew.

Just beyond the little village of Dunkineely I took a left turning which brought me to the ancient church of Killaghtee, built and rebuilt again and again over the centuries. This is another of the most secret places of Donegal.

I stopped the car at a broken bridge and walked across

the fields to the ruins feeling much like Charles Kingsley did on a similar occasion:

When I walk in the fields I am oppressed now and then with an innate feeling that everything I see has a meaning if I could but understand it. And this feeling of being surrounded by truths I cannot grasp amounts to indescribable awe.

The real gem here is the extraordinary stone slab to the south-west of the church. At the top of this slab is a Greek cross carved inside a circle. At the very centre of the cross are two small concentric circles, while just below it is one of those beautiful threefoil knots said to symbolise the Blessed Trinity.

Here again I meet up with tantalising mystery. Why the Greek cross in such a remote corner of Donegal? Is it a grave with some Mediterranean connection? Or is it just the whim of an ancient stone-cutter to while away the time. The truthful answer here is that we simply do not know. Professionals try to provide answers but most of the time it is mere guesswork. The reality is that we know so very little about the mentality of the early Celtic Christians. Most of their artifacts which survive are real puzzles. We can make some attempt at putting a date on them, but beyond that is silence. They have with great success hidden their secrets from us.

The pillaged churchyard with its sad neglected graves gave me a strange awareness of the concept of death. Maybe it is because I am getting old that such thoughts slip into my mind so often. Every old person thinks about death but some try to push these thoughts out of the mind. That I think is unwise. It is far better to face up to it and if possible make friends with that grim old scoundrel, scythe on shoulder, who will one day beckon to us with his bony finger.

# THE SECRET PLACES OF DONEGAL

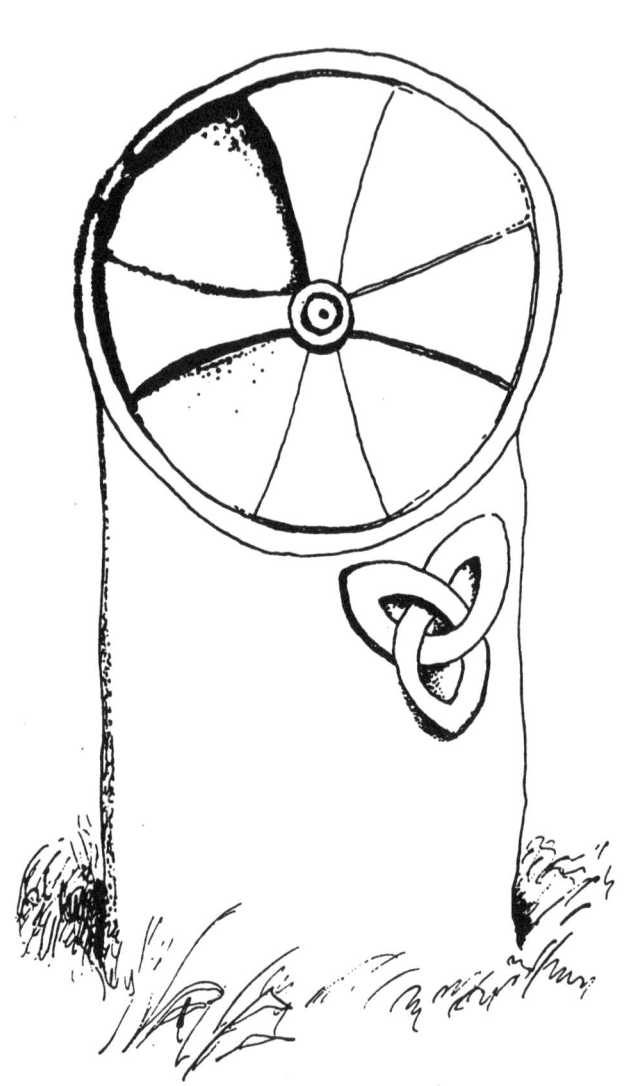

*Killaghtee*

# THE SECRET PLACES OF DONEGAL

There is still no answer to Hamlet's penetrating question: *To be or not to be*. But running away from it does not really help. Nevertheless I find it hard to accept that man's destiny is here among the rats, the worms and the nettles. This is hardly what we were born for. Man's fate is not generated in the body no more than electricity is generated in the wires. There is somewhere something infinitely greater and better. If Keats could say of the nightingale: 'Thou wast not born for death immortal bird', surely we can say, looking into the upturned innocent face of a child: 'Thou wast not born for death immortal one.'

Here in Killaghtee the briars and the weeds cover the bones of hundreds of human beings who lived as we live now, whose pulses beat, whose breath flowed freely, whose blood ran joyously through their veins, who laughed and cried, who loved and hated, who became successes or failures and who one day died. Is this the end? I do not think so.

When I got to Killybegs I went straight to the Catholic Church to see the painting of the Holy Family by Murillo described in the guide books. Unfortunately it had been taken away for safe-keeping so it was not on display.

Disappointed as I was I recalled the fate of another Murillo – in an Irish convent in a different part of the country – the value of which was reduced from hundreds of thousands to a few pounds when one of the nuns, on the orders of her superior, painted a purple knickers on the naked body of the infant Jesus. It was felt that the sight of a certain object might send strange thoughts prancing through the nuns' minds.

Killybegs' Catholic Church is a holy place of simplicity and dignity, a place that invites you to kneel and pray. Just inside the gates is a wonderful sculptured gravestone of

Niall Mór MacSweeney, a renowned warrior half Norse, half Scots-Celt. It was found at St John's Point and was erected here for safe-keeping. It is a superb piece of work, far more valuable in every way than even the Murillo.

They say that Rome is built on seven hills but that Killybegs is built on seven hundred hills. And for all the glory that is Rome, Killybegs, proportional to size, has as many if not more archaeological remains. Its name, *Na Cealla Beaga* the Small Cells, implies that it was once a great monastic centre. The whole countryside around is dotted with antiquities, and if you would like to spend some time exploring here I suggest you get Charles Conaghan's little book *History and Antiquities of Killybegs*. It is packed with valuable and accurate historical information that will very much enhance your visit.

One of the strangest things about Killybegs is the unusual cult of St Catherine that one runs across in many places. There are holy wells and churches named after her. Novenas and pilgrimages seeking her intercession have been regular events here for hundreds of years. Now the intriguing thing is that Catherine was a fourth century Egyptian saint.

It is said that she was a princess who faced the emperor Maximianus in AD 306 when she was only 18 and remonstrated with him for his cruelty to the Christians. For this he had her broken on the wheel and beheaded. Her body was brought to Mount Sinai where it was kept in a tomb in the church of the Blessed Virgin. This body exuded a holy oil for twelve hundred years and then stopped suddenly. During the centuries after her death her cult spread quickly throughout Europe. But how did it get to Killybegs and why did it not spread elsewhere in Ireland? The Killybegs people say that in the fifteenth century a Greek ship got into difficulties off the Donegal coast and was in danger of foundering. The captain and the crew appealed to St Catherine and promised to build a church in her honour if she saved them. She heeded their call and they landed safely in Killybegs. The sailors built a small church in her honour and called a well after her. All this, of course, may be pure legend but there must be some intelligent explanation for the strong link between this young Egyptian girl and the Donegal fishing village.

Killybegs harbour was a frequent port of call for ships of all nations. In 1602 a boat laden with salt landed there. As well as the salt two gentlemen who had been plotting against the British also landed there: Archbishop James O'Hely of Tuam and Bishop Neill O'Boyle of Raphoe. At once the British supergrasses in Killybegs reported:

They are hidden secretly and these seditious persons do so animate the people and dissuage them from their duties assuring the Irishry of a great foreign power to be coming.

It was here in Killybegs in 1600 that O'Neill and O'Donnell met the Spanish ambassador Ferdinand de Baranova and agreed to land a Spanish force in Killybegs. Unfortunately the Archbishop of Dublin wanted the force landed in Munster and he got his way despite the best military advice to the contrary. That is how they came to land in Kinsale. It is said that the Archbishop disapproved of the morals of O'Neill and O'Donnell and felt that the people of Munster, being better Catholics, deserved the honour of a Spanish landing. What in heaven's name all that had to do with military strategy is beyond me.

There is also a record of a British Captain Butler who wrote to the Lord Deputy from Killybegs as follows:

... I was forced around Ireland by a gale and so crippled by sickness that I had to throw overboard eighty men.

Not exactly the kind of gentleman one would like to have as one's companion on a cruise.

But Killybegs was not always a harbour of sadness. In 1627 the notorious Dutch pirate Claas Clampian landed there to take on water and food. It is also recorded that he took on about twenty Donegal prostitutes for an evening's entertainment. Some trouble broke out on board because the crew could only speak Dutch while the ladies could only speak Irish. The result of the night's carousing was: three drowned, twenty-one confined to quarters with various head wounds, six missing, while all the ladies came home safe and sound. It is said that Clampian swore he would never land in Killybegs again.

Today Killybegs is a thriving fishing harbour and no longer a centre of international political intrigue or riotious nights aboard pirate ships.

A short distance westward of Killybegs there is a little place called Shalwey and here I detoured along the coast road which is a delightful drive with magnificent views of land, sea and mountains dotted with little thatched cottages tottering towards the shore. Almost anywhere along here you can rest and relax as you watch the heaving restless seas burst into foam against the rugged cliffs. All around you are many more secret places where you can pause, take a stroll, meditate and think.

Just outside Kilcar one can make another delightful detour around Teelin Bay and on into Carrick. Most of the guide books give detailed accounts of how to get a breathless view of Europe's largest cliffs by climbing Slieve League. I'm afraid this is not for me. It is both overwhelming and frightening. To enjoy scenery I need beauty coupled with peace and not beauty coupled with anxiety, which I get enough of in my life without seeking it out when I am on holidays. So you are quite welcome to risk your life by climbing Slieve League, traversing the 'One Man's Path' which is only two feet wide with a drop of two thousand feet on the seaward side. Freud postulated that there is in varying degrees in all of us what he calls an unconscious Death Wish. I'm afraid it's not very strong in me so I'll steer clear of this climb and instead pay a visit to the beautiful little church of St Columba in Carrick and say a prayer to St Christopher for those foolhardy enough to climb Slieve League that they may return safely to their loved ones, and if they do not, may their souls, and all the souls of the faithful departed rest in peace. Amen.

The whole area of south-west Donegal is an area of extraordinary scenic beauty but there is another beauty which is hidden and which can only be experienced if one lays aside the trappings of tourism, moves among the ordinary people and wins a little of their confidence. This hidden beauty is the richness of their folklore and folk traditions.

There is scarcely a cottage in this whole area that is not alive with tales and stories, some more than a thousand years old – tales of fairies who stole human beings, of banshees who warned of death, witches who cast spells, mermaids who loved humans, kings and princes, as well as men and women with the evil eye. They have been told at firesides generation after generation and neither radio nor television has been able to silence them.

The best introduction to this aspect of Donegal life is a book called *Fairy Legends from Donegal* by Seán Ó hEochaidh, Máire Mac Neill and Seamas Ó Catháin. This book contains one hundred and thirty-six fairy legends full of suspense, mystery, humour and perhaps most of all, charm. These stories are published exactly as they were taken down from the lips of some of the best storytellers of Donegal. A knowledge of these stories can be a great discussion point with which to begin a conversation. Do not be surprised if you find out that they really believe that fairies, witches and banshees exist. Perhaps they do! Indeed I once met a local man who told me, over a pint, that he gave a banshee a cure for constipation and in return she gave him a tip for the Grand National and the horse won at 20 to 1!

Anyway I wish you the best of luck. If you succeed you will have penetrated and experienced the real depths of Donegal.

The road from Carrick to Glencolumbkille runs through untamed moorland and bog covered in purple heather. I stopped the car and took Misty for a walk through the wild loneliness. The words of the poem by William A. Byrne which I learned as a schoolboy came slowly across the years:

>     The purple heather is a cloak
>         God gave the bogland brown.
>     As men have made a pall of smoke
>         To lay about the town.
>
>     Our nights are long and rich in change
>         Unscreened by hill or spire,
>     From primrose dawn a lovely range
>         To sunset's farewell fire.
>
>     The reeds that pine about the pools
>         In wind and windless weather
>     The bees that have no singing rules
>         Except to sing together.
>
>     Then we have rest, so sweet, so good
>         The quiet rest you crave
>     The long deep bogland solitude
>         That fits a forest's grave.

## BUNDORAN – GLENCOLUMCILLE

High above in the sky a lark dropped golden chords of exquisite music on to the purple heather:

> Dear thoughts are in my mind
> And my soul soars enchanted
> As I hear the sweet lark sing
> In the clear air of the day.

It is in moments such as this that I feel we live in a marvellous world. In the quiet moments of a holiday we get a glimpse of what we are missing in our rushed life. We may learn to pause and listen, not only for the music outside but for the inner music of the soul which harmonises with it. We will then see there is no real division between ourselves and the beauty of the universe. The infinite cannot be divided against itself.

I made my way down a little road that twists and turns through the old-world village of Malinbeg. A short walk across the fields brought me to the remote and beautiful Silver Strand. It is hard to find words to describe the Silver Strand. Its wild untamed beauty makes one feel that if heaven does not begin here it does not begin on earth at all. Here in this solitude you can rest, relax, meditate and pray – or if circumstances are such 'whisper sweet nothings' into the ear of a loved one. Here Time stands still. Here you can feel peace when the heart is faint and hope seems gone. Here you can set a courageous face to the future, but it is really better to experience the glorious present: sand, sea, air, birds and beauty all around. The present is the only reality we know. The dead past is gone. A most merciful God has veiled the future from us. It is one of the kindest of all his mercies.

I lay down on the fresh clean sand with Misty by my side. It was a glorious summer's day – the kind of day that makes old men feel sixteen on the threshold of a first love.

## THE SECRET PLACES OF DONEGAL

The sky was full of a soft light and seemed to be caressed by wisps of fairy cloud. The seagulls were gliding motionless as if they were made of glistening spray and sunshine. I relaxed my body and mind and soon arrived at that state of pure being where all ego-yapping ceased and I moved into a realm of tranquillity, beyond thought, even beyond time.

'In a rest which is meditative and attentive,' wrote Amiel, 'the wrinkles of the soul are smoothed away and the soul itself spreads, unfolds and springs afresh, and like the trodden grass of the roadside, or the bruised leaf of a plant, repairs its injuries, becomes new, spontaneous, true and original.' Yet Homer sounded a word of caution: 'Like the lives of leaves are the lives of men.'

Nearly an hour later I aroused myself and went for a walk along the edge of the tide. Misty delighted himself jumping in and out in the freshness of the water, sometimes running from the waves, sometimes rolling in the sand. Then he settled down to a more cocky kind of trot, like a Dublin yuppie going to a convention.

Presently I noticed him sniffing at some object near the edge of the water. It was a baby seal, two feet long and it was dead. I examined the little body and found a bullet-hole in its head. What twisted perverted human being did this? What vile sickness within his soul made him raise his gun, take aim and kill this helpless little creature of God? What terrible evil lurks within the soul of man that makes him the only species that kills for pleasure and kicks?

Even in death the little agonised bloodstained face looked up appealingly at me. The tide was ebbing. I took off my trousers, caring not if anyone saw me and waded out as far as I could go with the helpless, lifeless body in my arms. I gently slipped it into the water and let it drift with the ebb, away out into the vast ocean where it would be among friends, far far away from the savagery of humans.

'Stand still,' counselled the psalmist, 'and consider the wondrous works of God.' Why do we have to do it with a loaded rifle in our hands and brutality in our hearts?

# TWO

# GLENCOLUMBKILLE – ANNAGRY

> *There is a famine abroad – a famine not of bread nor of gold but a famine of really great men. We are starved with mediocrity, we are dying of ordinariness. We are perishing of pettiness.*
>
> FR JAMES McDYER

The valley of Glencolumbkille must surely be one of God's masterpieces in Ireland. It is set into the landscape like a dew-drop on a morning rose. 'God was in good form the day he made it,' an old Donegal woman with a twinkle in her eye told me. The touching words of Dora Sigerson Shorter, while unlikely to appeal to today's frothy copiers of Joyce and Beckett, capture its simple beauty:

> 'Twas the dream of a God
> And the mould of his hand
> That you shook 'neath His stroke
> That you trembled and broke
> To this beautiful land.

As I parked the car near Doon Point and rested by the

## GLENCOLUMBKILLE – ANNAGRY

side of the road and contemplated the reposeful landscape the thought occurred to me that it may well have been the combination of its beauty and isolation which attracted our first strange ancestors to Glencolumbkille nearly six thousand years ago.

We know almost nothing of these people or of what they were like. The only remains they left behind them are cairns and dolmens which orthodox thinking proclaimed to be burial sites. There is little evidence for this. Those that have been excavated have shown few human bones and the truth is that we really do not know what they were. Mystery surrounds every one of them.

The discovery of such things as finely wrought gold objects, cells of batteries, pieces of computers, parts of planes and various types of electrical equipment embedded in rocks millions of years old and at depths of up to sixty feet below the earth's surface has set the cat among the archaeological pigeons. These artifacts have been given the name 'ooparts', a derivation of the words 'out-of-place' artifacts. This is because they have been found in conditions and places where they should not be according to our thinking, and they are now baffling top world scientists. But they are realities, so it may well be that our thinking is far off beam. Von Daniken and other writers suggested that they may have come from outer space but since the material they are made of is known earthly material, and not outer space material, it is hard to accept that viewpoint.

Scientists are now studying the theory that scores of thousands of years ago there existed a civilisation on earth which was light years ahead of ours and that some enormous geological calamity wiped it out. What that calamity was is unknown, but rather intriguing is the fact that the old biblical story of the Flood, which has.been treated with derision for so long, is now being seriously examined by scientists.

One cannot dismiss all this lightly simply because our minds have been programmed in a different direction. Unfortunately a lot of archaeological and anthropological thinking in Ireland is half-a-century behind world thinking, so while not accepting every foolish theory, we should at least try to keep an open mind. Other than the 'ooparts', there are, however, many unanswered questions which have been quietly shelved.

A number of skulls of prehistoric people called Khurits in Armenia showed evidence of top class surgery even by today's standards. Who were these surgeons of 4,000 years ago and where did they learn their skills? Professor Jagharian of the Erivan Medical Institute commented: 'We have found 4,000 year old obsidian razors at Lake Sevan that are so sharp that they can still be used today. Considering the ancient tools the doctors had to work with, I would say they were technically superior to modern-day surgeons.' Another skull thousands of years old, now in the Museum of Natural History, London, was found in Rhodesia sixty feet below the earth's surface with a bullet wound. Where did the bullet and gun come from?

There are scores of examples of such extraordinary mysteries given in various scholarly journals and books, like Rene Noorbergen's excellent *Secrets of the Lost Races*. A study of these documents gives one a very healthy scepticism towards the theories we have been taught concerning the evolution and development of the human race and the exact functions of the cairns, dolmens and standing stones. The simple truth is we can only hazard a guess and your guess could be as good as anyone else's.

So you can have a field day here in Glencolumbkille. The place is full of objects of mystery and poses many unanswered questions. So get to work. You might achieve fame and fortune by solving some. First of all read Fr McDyer's little guide *The Riches of Glencolumbkille*. This pinpoints every site and will be of invaluable help in locating them. Keep an open mind, however, and work out your own answers. If you do you will enjoy a real worthwhile holiday in one of the most secret places of Donegal. But a word of warning – beware of practical jokers!

One day many years ago when I was rambling among the lanes and little fields of Glencolumbkille I accidentally ran across a group of American tourists being lectured by a young man, not a local, who apparently had offered his services as an unofficial guide. I unobtrusively joined the group and while I did not add to my archaeological knowledge I had some great moments of enjoyment. The young man spotted that I was not an American tourist and from time to time he gave me a sly wink. He explained that these stones were ancient phallic symbols standing in full glory, drawing energy from the sun. This energy was stored in the stones and transmitted to men and women who were having marital problems such as impotence, frigidity, etc. The conditions were that the petitioner put his or her arms around the stones and say three Hail Mary's for the Pope's intentions. It would even be better if a man and woman put their arms around opposite sides of the stones together. The energy would then flow from the stones into the petitioners. Their problems would vanish and they would live happily ever afterwards.

The dolmens were also phallic symbols, he said, because if you half closed your eyes and examined them from a distance in various directions you could detect the outlines of different positions of love. Such knowledge was a great aid to marital bliss. After all, he said, you don't eat pig's head and cabbage every day. You need a little variety from time to time. The Americans were staring open-mouthed at him. At that moment he thanked them profusely for their attention and promised them practical and lasting results. When he finished a hat was discreetly passed through the crowd and although I did not contribute I noticed that it held quite a respectable quantity of notes.

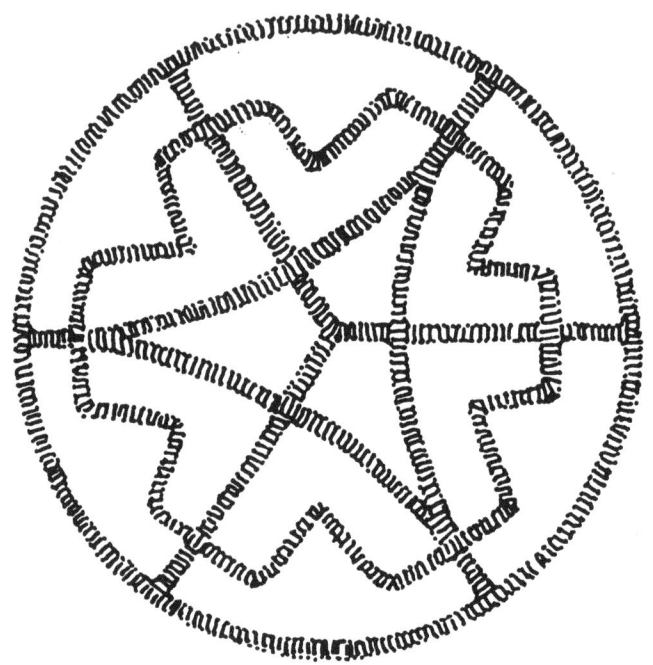

*From a slab at Glencolumbkille*

Later that summer I saw the same gentleman lecturing Americans at another site in a different part of the country and giving the high crosses an interpretation which the makers certainly did not intend.

The moral from this is that all in Glencolumbkille is not serious. You can enjoy a little fun too and if on your travels through Ireland you come across this lecturer enlightening a group of Americans, do not blow the gaff on him. After all everyone must try to live and who really knows? He might be a public benefactor rendering sensitive assistance to those who need it and the Americans surely won't miss a few dollars!

Not so many years ago Glencolumbkille was a small backward, under-developed parish unknown to all but the few who came occasionally to study its archaeological remains. Today it is spoken of and discussed not only throughout Ireland but also in many parts of Europe as a model of what determination can do. That change was brought about by the vision, ideals and leadership of one man, Father James McDyer.

In 1951 he was appointed curate in Glencolumbkille at a time when the morale of the people had reached an all-time low. The effects of centuries of oppression were visible all around. In his *Autobiography* he recalls:

Since the first British army arrived in Ireland, there has been violence, bloodshed, death, persecution, hatred, deprivation, poverty and exile. They banned the education of the Irish and then they sneered at us for our ignorance; they outlawed our religion and they hunted our priests down like dogs; and perhaps the greatest and most enduring indignity of all – they cleared the Irish from large tracts of their native soil. . . and planted their hostile colonists. . .

When he arrived in Glencolumbkille he saw a whole valley dying from neglect. He again recalls:

The vitality of the community was ebbing fast. When I settled in as curate at the beginning of 1952 and for several years afterwards the marriage rate hardly ever exceeded four or five marriages per annum. . . On reaching the age of sixteen or seventeen about eighty per cent of the boys and girls were emigrating. . . The population was resolving itself into the old and the very young and it was clear that before very long we would only have the old. . .

A fierce resolve gripped my mind. Perhaps I was influenced by the doughty cliffs that surrounded me. . . But certainly I am sure that I was moulded by the injustice that had been done to our people over the centuries. . . I was not so naive that I thought I could put at right the wrongs of a nation but I felt that I could add a little bit of stimulus to self-help which could arouse other isolated communities across the land.

Father McDyer identified what he called *The Five Curses of Glencolumbkille*. They were: no industry, no electricity, no public water supply, unsurfaced roads and no dispensary. He set about tackling each of these in turn. Of course like all great men he ran into plenty of opposition. It came largely from two sources: the indifference of certain sections of the people and the dead hand of bureaucracy. Centuries of opposition had so demoralised many people that they could not recognise the revolution taking place before their eyes. Many had come to love their slavery. It took a long time to convince these but in the end most of them were won over.

Officialdom was a much more deadly type of opposition because it very often pretended to be helpful. The drug of procrastination was administered liberally in the affairs of Glencolumbkille with the result that more than one first-class workable scheme never even got off the ground. Father McDyer himself said, 'it is better to stop cursing the dark and light ten candles even if half of them blow out.' Far less than half of them blew out in Glencolumbkille and the chances are that none of them would have blown out if officialdom had been more helpful.

The results of his years in Glencolumbkille were: community hall opened, agricultural show held, electricity switched on, roads re-surfaced, piped water scheme, folk museum opened, holiday village opened, four factories opened, emigration halted. Most important of all, he and his small band of devoted helpers gave the people of Glencolumbkille a pride in themselves and in their little valley. They could now hold their heads on high.

Father McDyer retired and went to live in Carrick. When I was writing this book he very kindly received me in his small compact bungalow. An air of absolute sincerity surrounded him. He had lost none of his idealism or enthusiasm and I formed the opinion that, in spite of his advancing years, if the occasion arose he would start all over again. One unusual remark he made was to the effect that as he got older he tended to see the Provisional IRA as having right on their side. The political parties he saw as purely opportunist.

I suggested that he write a new book dealing with the role of a parish priest, a book that would cover all aspects of the priest's activities within his parish, not only spiritual but cultural and economic as well. The book would be called *The Priest in the Parish*. He grasped this idea with enthusiasm and subsquently wrote me a number of letters about it.

Alas, it was not to be. A few months later he died peacefully in his chair. Here one could adapt the words of Horatio:

> Now cracks a noble heart.
> Goodnight, dear priest, and flights of angels
> Sing thee to thy rest.

On the road to Ardara I took a left turning along a narrow twisting by-way to a little village called Port. Despite the extraordinary beauty of cliff, stream and sea it is pervaded by a sense of tragedy. Port is a deserted village of ruined houses and broken hopes. In the 1940s the families left one by one because they had no future and could get no help from the government to develop their national resources. It was the time De Valera made his famous speech *The Ireland We Desire*:

That Ireland which we dreamed of would be the home of a people who valued material wealth only as the basis of right living, of a people who were satisfied with frugal comfort and devoted their leisure to things of the spirit – a land whose countryside would be bright with cosy homesteads, whose fields and villages would be joyous with the sounds of industry, with the romping of sturdy children, the contests of athletic youths and the laughter of comely maidens, whose firesides would be the forums for wisdom of serene old age.

There is nothing wrong with that vision of Ireland. It is certainly light years ahead of the yuppie Ireland of today. What is wrong is that while De Valera was making that speech Port, and other villages like it, were disintegrating mainly because he would not give them any help. Although De Valera was head and shoulders above those who followed him he cannot escape the charge that he was one of the great verbalisers in Irish history – a man for whom the notion of 'Principle without Practice' permeated much of his thinking, 'say out loud what should be done – and never do it'. As I sat there in this tragic atmosphere I fell to contemplating the unbelievably low level of leadership in Irish politics.

In the sixty-five years of the existence of the state our record of great leaders is very poor. Michael Collins was the only leader of top quality to emerge. De Valera, brilliantly tough in dealing with the British, reached his high point in his masterly reply to Churchill in 1945 when every Irish man and woman had reason to be proud of him. After that he steadily declined and ended his days a truly tragic figure having sided with those who abandoned the people of the six counties to their terrible fate. Apart from Seán MacBride, who never got a real chance, most of the others were men of impeccable mediocrity.

Lemass became obsessed with the notions of grandeur and started the process of bringing us into the EEC. This process was completed by Lynch. When we joined the EEC we had 50,000 unemployed. Now we have 250,000 and still rising. Haughey has shown himself one of the weakest so far – pathetically incapable of standing up to the British. As I write these lines our ex-Taoisigh cost the taxpaper nearly £100,000 each every year between benefits-in-kind and pension. Are they worth it? What could be done in places like Port with that kind of money? How many tears, hurts and heartaches could be saved?

It seems as if we in Ireland still await our De Gaulle, Adenauer or Gasperri – or indeed our Margaret Thatcher. We resemble a rudderless ship in a storm, flying the Union Jack instead of the Tricolour. In the meantime, Port and other such places in Ireland are a tragic reminder of the poor quality of the politicians we elect to lead us.

Anyway, let us get away from this depressing theme – away to the beauty of Donegal.

It is almost impossible to describe the road from Glencolumbkille to Ardara without running out of superlatives. Mountain, lake, river, moorland, isolation, solitude, seclusion – it's all there, especially as you drive through the extraordinary Alpine pass of Glengesh. Here you will find scenery not a distraction but an inspiration, with secret places behind every wall and every rock and every bush. This is one of the most stimulating drives in Donegal.

Just before I got to Ardara I took a left turning for the hamlet of Maghera. This is a delightful drive and it has not yet been discovered by too many tourists. About two miles along this road there is another penal Mass rock, where I paused for a few minutes and visualised the scene as it was during those terrible days: the group of ragged, barefooted men, women and children who had trudged over mountain and hill in rain, hail and snow to worship their God: the priest saying Mass on the old rock with a flour-sack as an altar-cloth and two sticks tied together to make a cross: up on the hills a few look-out men scanning the countryside for the British soldiers. Yet despite the great sense of tragedy there must also have been a great sense of peace – *Where two or three are gathered in My name I am also with them.*

Near the delightful old-world village of Maghera is the magnificent Essaranka waterfall and beyond the village a wild and lonesome glen with the Owenwee river cascading its way down to the sea. Here is a secret place where one can sit and contemplate and, as Donegal people say, 'make your soul'.

Ardara village, set on high ground with a magnificent view of the countryside, is a renowned centre for homespuns and crafts. These are tastefully presented in many shops at attractive prices and the visitor need not be afraid that he or she will be ripped off. In the church is a strikingly beautiful and inspiring Evie Hone window. This is seen at its best in the early evening when the setting sun filters through and fills the church with its multi-coloured rays.

It is known as the Rose Window from its shape and it depicts Christ among the doctors. When Evie Hone became a Catholic she concentrated largely on religious art for the rest of her life. She has created more than seventy stained-glass windows for churches all over the country.

A few miles to the east of Ardara is the little town of Glenties, clean, tidy and well laid out. After a delightful lunch in a pub of character, I stolled up to the church to

## GLENCOLUMBKILLE – ANNAGRY

visit the grave of one of the greatest of all Donegal men, Canon James McFadden. For an entire lifetime he fought landlordism, injustice, oppression and exploitation of the poor. He suffered imprisonment, humiliation, harassment and privation but the British could not break his spirit and he lived to see the whole rotten system eventually destroyed.

In his day the Glenties was largely Irish-speaking and, unlike so many other clerics who toadied to the British, he conducted his pastoral duties through the medium of Irish. Of all the people associated with the Glenties he was the giant. Here he rests amongst those simple people he fought so hard for and gave so much of his life.

At the head of Gweebarra Bay is the little hamlet of Lettermacaward which is truly another of Donegal's most secret places. Here I stopped and spent half-a-day rambling around this charming and historic countryside armed with Karl Cannon's excellent little book *A Tour of Lettermacaward*. The name itself has many meanings but I think it means Hillside of the Son of the Ward, the Ward being the poet of the O'Donnell clan. The writer Patrick McGill was born near here and through his naavy recitations he became a kind of an Irish Robert W. Service. He wrote a few minor novels some of which were unfortunately spoiled by bitterness. He plummeted in the affections of the Donegal people when he joined the British army at a time when Ireland was engaged in a life and death struggle with that army. Nevertheless he did try to speak for the poor and lowly:

> I do not sing
> of plaster saints or jealous gods
> But of the little ones I know
> Who paint their cheeks or bear their hods
> because they live in doing so
> The hapless life on earth below.

# THE SECRET PLACES OF DONEGAL

Not far off the road near Trusklieve Hill there seems to have been quite a large monastic settlement, but all that is left now is a small slab with an inscribed cross. It is said that in the early part of this century a local dug up this slab and used it as a lintel in a house he was building. However when he returned the next day all the walls were knocked and the slab was back in its original position – a warning to all would-be treasure hunters to keep away from Lettermacaward.

Don't forget to call into Melly's Bar if you have a mind to quench your thirst. This is a delightful friendly hostelry and the family will be only too glad to help you in any way they can. Local tradition says that in the early part of the nineteenth century this bar was owned by a Dunleavy family. They were cursed by a priest, who foretold that their name would die out in the area. The reason for this curse was that during the famine it was alleged that they mixed horse manure with the porridge which they then sold to the starving people. Whether or not that is true it is a good story and a lot of writers believe that you should never spoil a good story for the sake of truth!

Gweebarra Bay marks the beginning of that part of Donegal which many believe to be the real Donegal – the Rosses. As I drove along the road to Dungloe I turned on the radio to hear the news and instead I heard a recording of John McCormack singing *By the Short Cut to the Rosses*:

> By the short cut to the Rosses a fairy girl I met
> I was taken in her beauty as a fish is in a net
> The fern uncurled to look at her, so very fair was she
> With her hair as bright as seaweed new-drawn from out the sea.
>
> By the short cut to the Rosses ('twas on the first of May)
> I heard two fairies piping, and they piped my heart away

## GLENCOLUMBKILLE – ANNAGRY

They piped 'till I was mad with joy, but when I was alone
I found my heart was piped away and in my breast a stone.

This really set the mood for the Rosses, the rugged, barren home of the Gael. Fairies do not seem a bit out of place here. In fact you could meet one anywhere. When I was a boy I always longed to meet the fairy girl of my dream and I wouldn't mind a bit my heart being piped away. It's an unpredictable kind of organ, anyway, that has landed me in the height of trouble more often than I can count. So far, these Titians have eluded me, but sure there's no harm in hoping.

The little town of Dungloe brings to mind immediately that giant of the Irish economic scene, Paddy Gallagher, better known as Paddy the Cope. In physical appearance Paddy was far from being a giant. He was a low-sized, chubby little man whose face bubbled with laughter and fun. Yet behind that jovial exterior there ticked one of the sharpest and ablest brains this country has ever known. Paddy was one of those great Irishmen, like General Costello and C. S. Andrews, who built up this nation and who showed the world that Irishmen could do it. I knew all three of them, although I only met Paddy a few times. They were men of strong nationalistic outlook who loved their country deeply and who utilised unselfishly their great talents to help the Irish people because, they believed, a nation was its people. 'The morale is to the physical as three is to one,' said Napoleon. They had the morale and they had the gift of inspiring it in others. They did not suffer fools gladly and I am constantly intrigued by thoughts of how they would deal with some of the managerial yuppies and their jargon – the very enthronment of mediocrity, floundering in the Irish economic scene today.

*Paddy The Cope*

Paddy the Cope had no degree in business studies or in economics. He did not attend any of the best colleges. It is most unlikely that he would pass an interview test for any important job in Irish industry. Yet in the co-operative movement he built up a mighty organisation that employs hundreds of people and he has been emulated all over the world. He was educated at a local national school by a wonderful schoolmaster called Mickey Neddy. Mickey realised the kind of tough world his pupils were destined for and he ignored the official syllabus and taught them how to read, write and count. But over and above these he taught them how to fight with their fists and how to deal with people who insulted them. Mickey demonstrated this practically when he upended a Department of Education school inspector with a belt in the jaw for making disparaging remarks about his pupils.

Paddy the Cope left school at twelve years of age able to read, write, count and fight. He walked twenty and thirty miles to hiring fairs and hired himself out to farmers for £1 per month. His wonderful book called *My Story* by Paddy the Cope tells the story of his life, his early struggles, his founding of the co-operative movement. Writing on his life and work Dr E. P. McDermott says:

It is a book of an unlettered man, a man who just knows how to read and write but a man that talks straight out from his heart. . .
Paddy is a symbol of the age, of self-reliance and of co-operation. His story is the story of the Irish people taking their destiny into their own hands. It is a clarion call to hope, to perseverance and to progress. To the very midst of the barren rocks and brown

boglands, and to a poor and uneducated people he has brought prosperity. . .

It is quite intriguing that no official honour or recognition was ever given to men like Paddy the Cope, Father McDyer or General Costello. Some Taoiseach could have nominated them to the Senate but there their sincerity might be out of place in that ineffective, garrulous body. Some university might have conferred honorary degrees on them but again, in view of some who have had degrees conferred; they might not be too anxious to join that company.

One of the qualities which saturated these great men through and through was their deep and abiding patriotism. They were thoroughly unlike many of the present breed of Irish leadership who resemble the bookies' tick-tack men on a race-course more than leaders. They never went on their knees begging the British to please honour them with a spit. They were proud to be Irish and it was this very pride which was their great strength. In so far as I knew them they were devoid of personal ambition or greed. The good of the country and of its people came first in their lives.

Costello I knew best of all. For many years I worked with him in the army and in all that time I never knew him, even once, to put personal advantage before duty. Because of his popularity, ability and integrity he was regarded with grave suspicion by many senior politicians. Fearing only for themselves, they harboured the idea that he might lead a revolt and take over the country. This possibility was openly discussed, even within the army itself, but I am quite certain that it was the farthest thought from Costello's mind. He was much too loyal an Irishman to even contemplate any such action. Although he bitterly attacked some of my writings, both in public and in private, I cannot allow that to blind my judgement that he was one of the three or four greatest Irishmen of this century.

The fishing village of Burtonport lies a few miles northwest of Dungloe and if the wind is from a westerly direction you can smell it long before you reach it. If Bord Fáilte were offering a prize for the untidiest village in Ireland Burtonport would be well in the running. Apart from the smell of stinking fish, the area near the sea is littered with old rope, fragments of timber, discarded nets, parts of engines, broken fish boxes, etc, all rotting away, and coloured by a variety of plastic bags and bottles of various shapes and sizes. Surely some local group could come together and remedy this unsightly chaos.

I was met on the pier by Finn Costello who lives on Innisfree and who very kindly offered to bring me across to the island in his boat. The sun was shining brightly as we travelled through a kind of summer haze of transparent softness to this enchanted isle.

Innisfree is the home of a community called the 'Screamers'. They live in several cottages on the island and they are about 80% self-sufficient. They are vegetarians who grow their own food, make their own bread, cheese and butter and generally try to live as much as possible off the natural resources of the island. They are anti-nuclear, anti-war and anti-pollution, but not anti-love.

The name 'Screamers' was unfairly applied to them because they practise a therapeutical system which advocates the release of emotions rather than their suppression. If they are upset they cry openly. If they are angry they scream and prance about. If they are happy they jump and shout for joy. In this way they find their real selves.

Those who would say that this is all nonsense might usefully study the latest techniques in Japanese management which advocate exactly such a therapy. Indeed major Japanese companies now provide special gymnasiums so that their employees can work out their emotions in this way – even going so far as to make rubber effigies of top management so that the workers can punch them with their fists. The Japanese management system is reckoned to be the best in the world so we may well have a great deal to learn on Innisfree.

There is something else we might usefully look at on Innisfree. If their vegetarianism and self-sufficiency methods were applied to the whole country unemployment would be wiped out, we could support double or treble our present population and at the same time become one of the richest countries in the world. This is a scientific fact based on the optimum output of food per acre of land as between meat, vegetables and grain.

However some criticism has been levelled against them for their free attitude to sex. I am always inclined to view most such critics with great caution, and to suggest to them that they might usefully read Somerset Maugham's short story *Rain*. Sex is a very personal thing and what two consenting adults do or do not is their own affair. It often happens that those who protest loudest have deep-rooted sexual problems themselves. If sex can make you laugh, they say, it is usually pretty harmless. If it cannot then there may well be clouds on the horizon. Anyway the slaughter of two world wars was not caused by sexual freedom.

When we reached the small harbour we took one of the little crooked paths which wound its way to Finn's cottage where I was made welcome by his wife Mary. Soon word got around that there was a stranger on the island and one by one occupants of the other cottages dropped in. I was glad that I had brought a little gift of a few bottles of wine with me. It seemed to fill us with lightheartedness, loosen our tongues and give wings of freedom to our conversation.

In the short two hours I was there we discussed a vast variety of subjects: child-rearing, the legal system, marriage, divorce, hot-water bottles, espionage, organic gardening, family fights, cutting turf, paring corns, international banking, curing boils, sex in the army, the dole, venereal disease, reminiscences of youth and a host of other subjects. Indeed instead of they shocking me I think it was I who shocked them.

I was quite conscious of the fact that I had had a most wonderful and stimulating afternoon and I could not help comparing it with what would have happened had I gone instead for afternoon tea to a middle-class Dublin 4 family of impregnable virtue.

Straightaway I would find myself in a mental prison, handcuffed to conventionality. I would have to be dressed in a certain careless way – the phrase is I believe 'casual wear' – to show that I was ever so slightly avant garde, since that is fashionable nowadays amongst the plastic men and women of television diet. More than likely the tea would be presided over by a woman who during her life devoured those around her and whose waist showed all the signs of it. My conversation would be extremely restricted: the latest chat show on television, the adulation of some of the presenters, the best restaurants where the science of the gullet could be satisfied, the most exclusive resorts for holidays, not in Ireland of course, the enumeration of important people we had recently met, and we might indulge in a little of the *risque* by discussing the brand of toilet paper used by Fergie and Di. Please do not misunderstand me and think I am sneering at this way of life. I am not. Everybody is entitled to his or her own lifestyle, and some find great pleasure in the plastic way of life. They are fully entitled to it. But what a contrast with Innisfree where the conversation cascaded and pranced like a mountain waterfall after fresh summer rain. When after my short stay I left the island I felt saddened as if I were leaving old and trusted friends.

I went north from Burtonport and made a little diversion to the left out to Cruit island. It is really not an island since it is connected to the mainland by a bridge. Cruit island is another of the secret places of Donegal. Here you have magnificent peaceful beaches, usually uncrowded. It is also a great place for holy wells, which a local cynic told me are being added to every year! So if you have a shovel handy you could dig one for yourself. Scatter a few ribbons and medals around and no doubt some archaeologist will find a connection between it and Balor of the Evil Eye.

There is also a large slab on Cruit island called An Leacht Mór which is said to cure illness if you sleep on it. I would imagine, however, if you could possibly sleep on it you couldn't be very sick. A thirsty talkative tourist, whom I met once in a pub, explained to me that the slab was really a fertility rock. For childless couples, he said, to exercise their conjugal rights here worked miracles. Indeed he was certain that scores of Donegal people owed their existence to a summer frolic on An Leacht Mór. So if you have a little problem it might be worth a try. It couldn't do much harm anyway.

East of Cruit island is the little village of Annagry where the people have a reputation for being tightlipped and uncommunicative. There is a story told of an Annagry man who, while on pilgrimage to Rome, attended a sermon preached by the Pope.

'What did he preach about?' he was asked when he came home.

'Sin.'

## THE SECRET PLACES OF DONEGAL

'What did he have to say about it?'
'I'd say he was against it,' was the laconic answer.

I did not find the people of Annagry particularly uncommunicative. Indeed they were most helpful to me when I enquired the way to the remote townsland of Kerrytown. I was given precise and exact directions which enabled me to find the place without trouble.

Kerrytown became famous during the Second World War, because the Blessed Virgin was supposed to have appeared many times there. According to local testimony she was a very beautiful lady in her early twenties. She wore a magnificent blue robe and a wreath of flowers on her head. She carried a curly-haired baby in her arms. She appeared several times to many people, including a very sceptical priest. Because of newspaper reports Kerrytown became a place of pilgrimage and thousands flocked there to pray especially on feastdays of the Blessed Virgin.

In later years the fervour seems to have eased off and the day I went to visit it it was deserted. An unusual framed picture of the Blessed Virgin was resting on a rock in the cliff and scattered around were some small statues, medals, money and ribbons. Yet as I sat alone in the heather, I felt a strange prayerful atmosphere all around the place – much more prayerful that I ever felt at Lourdes or Knock. A kind of an untroubled calm descended on my soul. It was as if there were no evil in the world – only immense goodness, like Eden before the fall.

I am not particularly enamoured of strange phenomena such as apparitions or moving statues, although I have seen a statue moving, but that was immediately after a convivial evening in the pub when one might say I was slightly prejudiced. Nevertheless if we accept the concept of an allpowerful God then we must accept also the concept of such apparitions and phenomena since not to do so is to put

## GLENCOLUMBKILLE – ANNAGRY

limits, determined by our own minds, to that limitless power of God. Our modern world is inclined to sneer at such strange happenings but it was not so in the past. In the early centuries after the death of Christ miracles were not seen in a particularly unusual light. In his book *The Decline and Fall of the Roman Empire* Gibbon, who was no friend of Christianity, recorded that the setting aside of what appeared to be the law of nature was by no means unusual. The blind got back their sight, the crippled walked, food was multiplied and the resurrection of the dead, was 'far from being an uncommon event'.

The Church, however, is particularly cautious about accepting such phenomena as apparitions. Firstly because of the possibility of bringing religion into disrepute, and secondly because of a slight professional jealousy that such apparitions are made manifest to the ordinary people and not to important people like bishops, cardinals and popes. This is seen as somewhat inconsiderate of God.

Whether or not there were apparitions at Kerrytown I cannot answer but this I do know: I have experienced a sense of peace here that I rarely experienced anywhere before. I found it to be one of those secret places in Donegal where time seemed to stand still and where human words are completely inadequate to convey the deep sense of calm, harmony and unity with all life that pervades the lonely landscape. Only a child, or a poet with the mind of a child, can capture it:

> The angels keep their ancient places
>   Turn but a stone, and start a wing;
> 'Tis ye, 'tis your estrangèd faces
>   That miss the many-splendoured thing.

Perhaps the most delightful story of an apparition was told to me by an old friend of mine, Larry the Liar, a tinker who dealt in kettles, pots and other scrap. I had known Larry for twenty years or more and in my travels through the country I often ran into him in the most unexpected places. The first time I met him was in a town in the midlands when he was not too anxious to meet the police. They wanted to ask him a few questions in connection with the disappearance of a pig's head from a butcher's shop. It was also suggested that he removed a pair of new stockings from a parish priest's clothes line and left his own stinking ones instead. I helped him out of the town without attracting the attention of the police and since then we were friends until his death. Larry was a tall, angular man with a bruised and battered face and a pair of long legs so out of joint that they looked like two crooked gate posts.

According to Larry the Blessed Virgin appeared to him in Donegal between Rathmullan and Rathmelton at a place called Brown Knowe made famous by the ballad *The Maid of the Sweet Brown Knowe*. He had just lit a fire of twigs to make a drop of tea. He was down on his knees coaxing the fire along with his hat when this beautiful lady appeared in front of him. He was, he said, struck with terror but she spoke very kindly and gently to him and said: 'Do not be afraid, Larry, I won't harm you. I am the Mother of God.'

'What do you want me to do, Your Blessedness?' asked Larry, now much relieved, as if meeting the Mother of God was an every day occurrence. 'Have you any message you want me to pass on?'

'I have indeed,' said the Blessed Virgin. 'Tell the people to stop doing penance and enjoy themselves more. Satan and his agents, the politicians, love penance and gloom and they have put more than enough of it in the world. The people should laugh and sing and dance and enjoy themselves in a good healthy way and if they do I will look after them.'

'I'll do that, Your Blessedness,' said Larry, 'but 'tis likely that a lot of people won't pay much attention to a tramp like me.'

'They didn't pay much attention to my Son either,' she said, 'but you can always start with yourself and enjoy yourself. Tell me, could you sing any old come-all-ye from the hills of Donegal?'

Larry, ever anxious to oblige, sang the most fitting song of all for the area: *The Maid of the Sweet Brown Knowe.*

> Come-all-ye lads and lassies
> And listen to me awhile.
> I will sing to you a verse or two
> That will cause you all to smile.
> 'Tis all about a young man
> I am going to tell you now
> How he lately came a-courting
> The Maid of the Sweet Brown Knowe.
>
> This young man said, 'my pretty maid
> Will you come along with me,
> We'll both run off together
> And married we will be.
> We'll join our hands in wedlock banns
> As I'm speaking to you now
> I will do my best endeavour
> For the Maid of the Sweet Brown Knowe.'
>
> This fair and fickle young thing
> She knew not what to say.
> Her eyes did shine like diamonds bright
> And merrily did play.
> She said, 'Young man, your love subdue
> For I'm not ready now.
> I'll tarry another season
> At the foot of the Sweet Brown Knowe.'

The young man says, 'My pretty maid
How can you answer so.
Look down in yonder valley
My crops do gently grow.
Look down in yonder valley
Where my horses and my plough
Are doing their daily labour
For the Maid of the Sweet Brown Knowe.'

'If they're doing their daily labour
Kind sir, 'tis not for me.
I've heard of your behaviour
I have indeed,' says she
'There is an inn where you call in
I hear the people say
Where you rap and you call and pay for all
And go home at the break of day.'

'If I rap and I call and pay for all
The money is all my own.
I will drink none of your fortune
For I hear that you've got none.
You thought you had my poor heart broke
When speaking to me now,
But I'll leave you where I found you
At the foot of the Sweet Brown Knowe.'

'More power to you, Larry,' said the Blessed Virgin clapping her hands with joy. 'I'd like to get the words of that ballad for St Joseph. He's a great collector of come-all-yes.'

'Well now, Your Blessedness,' said Larry, 'you might find it hard to believe but I have a bit of schoolin' and I learned to read and write when I was young and if you like I'll write down the words for you before you go, even though the spellin' mightn't be the best.'

'Not at all, Larry,' she answered. 'I can learn them off by heart. You see,' she added in a confidential whisper, 'I never learned to read or write.'

Larry told this story with gusto in hundreds of pubs throughout the country. His chest expanded as he recounted with pride how he had one up on the Queen of Heaven because he could read and write.

Each time he told the story he added that little extra bit of artistry to it. The last time I heard him tell it was many, many years ago shortly before he died. In this version the Blessed Virgin gave him full freedom to indulge in a little pick-pocketing at race meetings and to show the three card trick to drunken farmers at fairs. The theological basis for this was that in the next world those who helped themselves to the pickings at race-meetings or fairs are not punished. Only those stupid enough to have been taken in are punished. Stupidity and gullibility are grave sins.

Whether or not the Blessed Virgin appeared to Larry we do not know. But if she is the Queen of Heaven she must be all-powerful and can surely do what she likes. She might even learn to read and write.

THREE

# GWEEDORE – GARTAN

*Play me the music of things that are done rather then the music of things that are said.*

FINN MacCUMHAIL

'You are now entering the real Ireland,' a man told me in Crolly. 'This whole Gweedore area is what all Ireland was once like and what all Ireland should now be like: Irish speaking, prosperous and magnificent to look at.'

Everywhere I went the beautiful melifluous tones of the Irish language were all around me. I heard it spoken by shopkeepers, petrol pump attendants, road workers, farmers, and I even heard it spoken in a cemetery by the men opening a grave. Somewhere within me a sympathetic chord was touched and its echo returned back to my soul. All at once I felt as if I were one with them and that together we had jumped a thousand years of barbarianism and had found our real selves again, I cannot explain this feeling. I do not get it in other Irish-speaking areas but here in Gweedore it casts a spell over me. It was as if I had returned home after a long, long exile.

For several thousand years we have been expressing our

deepest thoughts in a language with a particularly distinctive vocabulary and with unique nuances and subtle shades of meaning. But in the last 300 years we have had to do an about turn and express ourselves in a completely alien language which did not evolve from ours but which was forced upon us by the sword. This, psychologists tell me, can have a serious and disturbing effect on the total personality. We have lost contact with our origins and with our cultural past. We are like orphans forced into a hostile poorhouse, like bewildered schizophrenics in a global mental home.

In the early years of this century a small farmer named McBride who came from this area was charged in court with having his name written in Irish on an ass's car. He was found guilty and fined. He appealed his case to the High Court in Dublin, and there was represented by a young barrister who was none other than Pádraig Pearse. Pearse argued that McBride lived in an area where only Irish was spoken, that he spoke hardly any English himself and that surely in these circumstances it was no offence to write his name in Irish. The case was heard by Lord Chief Justice O'Brien (Peter the Packer), Mr Justice Andrews and Mr Justice Gibson.

Their Lordships dismissed the appeal, poured scorn on Pearse and completely rejected the concept that Irish had any legal place in Ireland. The English language only was the language of Ireland. All that happened some eighty years ago. Is it possible that it could happen again today?

The destruction of the Irish language was, of course, a deliberate policy of the British, and was very important to them for two reasons. Firstly, the British surmised, when a people's language goes their soul goes with it. Secondly, by making English the language of Ireland the propaganda war became simpler.

The first task of the British was to create amongst the

Irish a mental attitude which said in effect: 'Irish is an inferior language and is no good.' They did this particularly in the eighteenth and nineteenth centuries by forcing English on the people and by making it the language of all departments of public life; the schools, the courts, parliament, local authorities, newspapers, books and every form of communication with the public. Children in the schools were punished for speaking Irish and there was no LFM (Language Freedom Movement) to defend them.

An interesting point here was the British belief that in time they could cease direct involvement because the Irish themselves would do the work for them. This was very shrewd and far-seeing political thinking. Over and over again the British were to make full use of this policy: get the Irish to destroy the Irish. In fact it was the Irish who destroyed the Irish language. One of the best examples here is that of Daniel O'Connell. He was a fluent Irish speaker and so were ninety per cent of his audiences but he persisted in addressing them in English and singing *God Save the Queen* at the end of his meetings. John Mitchel's description of him was terse and accurate:

Poor old Dan! Wonderful, mighty, jovial and mean old man! With silver tongue and smile of witchery and heart of unfathomable fraud. What a royal yet vulgar soul. . . the base servility of a hound and the cold cruelty of a spider. Think of the theory of moral and peaceful agitation, the most astounding organon of public swindling since man first bethought of obtaining money under false pretences.

O'Connell was, of course, ably supported by the Catholic hierarchy who, in return for a few crumbs of material advantage, threw their full weight behind the British effort and as long as the British kept feeding the crumbs, the hierarchy, like Pavlov's dogs, obeyed.

## GWEEDORE – GARTAN

By the time the twenty-six counties were given a measure of freedom in 1921 the Irish language was almost destroyed. Even at that late hour it could have been saved. Czechoslovakia, Hungary, Serbia, Rumania, Bulgaria, Greece and today Israel have saved their languages. The Spanish language survives in spite of hundreds of years of occupation by the Moors. Only Ireland failed – but worse was to follow. In 1921, 250,000 spoke Irish as their daily language. Today, after 65 years of native government, less than ten per cent of that number use it. It was left to a native Fine Gael coalition government to give it the final death wound by making it an non-essential subject in the educational curriculum and imposing upon the Irish people the eternal shame of knowing that we are the only country in the world where competence in one's native language is not mandatory. This was done without a pip squeak from Fianna Fáil, the party dedicated to restoring it. Is it any wonder that so many other countries see us as little better then a spineless fraud? Is this why they are so sure they can bully us into doing what they want?

Here in Gweedore the people have preserved their language, they use it despite the blinkered politicians and civil servants and while it may not be the only cause of material progress in Gweedore it is a major factor since it gives them the sense of identity so necessary to maintain their high morale.

Because of the poor standard of history teaching today it is not easy to realise what the Irish people, and particularly the people of Gweedore, had to endure during the latter half of the last century. The British landlord had absolute power over the tenant. He could be evicted at a whim whether or not he paid his rent. He could be evicted too if his daughter refused to go to bed with the landlord; or if he refused to send his children to a Protestant school; or he did not vote as he was directed. Like the six counties today the system of justice was largely corrupt. Out of 132 judges 114 were Protestant and of these eighty were landlords, twenty-five land agents, five military officers and two Protestant clergymen. The Irish tenant did not have much chance of justice.

The local landlord in Gweedore was Lord George Hill, a scoundrel and a tyrant of the first order who evicted tenants right, left and centre. The great Canon McFadden was parish priest and he fought Hill every inch of the way. McFadden was abused, harassed, arrested and later sentenced to six months in jail by a corrupt court. Having come out of jail he continued to struggle and lived to see the landlord system ruined.

In the whole sordid story, which is told by Proinsias Ó Gallchobhair in his *History of Landlordism in Donegal*, there were two bright flashes – when ordered to fire on fellow Irishmen a policeman named Thomas Haughey refused. He flung his rifle and equipment at his commanding officer's feet and resigned. (May I very respectfully suggest here that another more famous man of the same surname might usefully learn a lesson or two from this brave policeman).

A Constable McBride was asked to identify Canon McFadden at a funeral in Armagh so that he could be arrested. McBride refused and said: 'I am a peace-officer not a priest hunter,' and resigned forthwith. Again and again history repeats itself. In Ireland it was always the few – the very few – who defied tyranny.

Contrary to the 'pub-blather' which the tourist will constantly hear *we are not a great nation*. On the whole we are a rather worthless nation, saved by a wonderful minority – a minority as low as ten per cent of the population. The majority, which is really our sub-culture, have come to love their chains and delight in their 'downstairs' role. This is a vital key for those who wish to understand the Irish. The majority of our people, and especially some of our politicians and civil servants, are forever on their knees fawning and forelock-lifting.

In Bunbeg I dropped in to see two young friends of mine, the beautiful Gillespie sisters, Áine and Eileen, who are trying to rebuild their lives after spending ten terrible years in a British jail. Unfortunately the track record for many years shows that if you are Irish you have little chance of justice in British courts, especially at that time when the British were conducting show-trials of the Irish like Stalin's show-trials of the 1930s. Their well-written, sensitive, autobiography, *Sisters in Cells*, now translated from Irish, tells of the terrible suffering and humiliations they had to endure down to the final insensitive boorishness when, three months before they were due for release, they were refused parole to attend their father's funeral. This was to an extent softened by the wonderful reception which they got in Donegal towns on their return from jail. Their homecoming was triumphant. Cheering crowds lined the streets, bands played, speeches were made. Thousands welcomed them – a not-too-subtle comment on what the Donegal people thought of British justice.

The road from Bunbeg to Bloody Foreland is yet another of Donegal's pleasant meandering routes. All around one can experience enchanting views of sea, islands and mountain. If at all possible Bloody Foreland should be seen with the setting sun behind it. It was these extraordinary red sunsets that gave it its name and not, as one might think, any gory battle of the past.

A few miles west of Bloody Foreland is the delightful

strand of Magheroarty from where you can make arrangements to travel to Tory Island or Inishbofin. Tory Island is one of the secret places of Donegal but it is not a place you can explore in a day. Also it would take an entire book to describe the many wonders to be experienced on the island. The nearer island of Inishbofin is only 3 miles away and it is well worth a day trip. On the northern part of the island there is a stone cottage which was once the summer home of Professor Kingsley Porter, an American archaeologist, probably one of the greatest authorities on Irish high crosses. Porter was a wealthy man who had purchased Glenveagh Castle, but as it was a little far from the sea he had a stone cottage built on the most remote part of Inishbofin. Together with his wife Lucy he spent many summers in this most secret corner of Donegal.

A. Kingsley Porter

## GWEEDORE – GARTAN

In July 1933 tragedy struck. His wife, Lucy Porter describes what happened:

... in the morning he (Kingsley) had gone out ahead of me and it must have been to the cliffs above the sea and he must have drowned. And the spring tide ebbing (it was the time of the summer moon) and the strong offshore wind blowing, must have swept his body out to sea, while a storm had come up bringing thunder, lightning and rain. Although Owen, Pat (two fishermen) and I searched all day long and into the night we had found no trace of him. . . no physical sign of him was ever again to be found.

There has always been some element of mystery about Kingsley Porter's death. According to newspaper reports at the time he was drowned off Tory Island from a curragh. It seems strange that he should have gone so far away to Tory in a curragh without his wife knowing it. The mystery deepens if one pays attention to the rumour that years later he was seen in New York. Yet another story says that a jealous rival turned the cursing stones of Innishmurray against him. Whatever happened he disappeared and it may well be that only the wild lonely cliffs of Inishbofin hold the answer.

In Falcarragh and Gortahork we are in the very heart of the Irish speaking Ireland. Here amid this beautiful scenery large crowds of students come every summer to learn the language. This is something which is a phenomenon of recent years – a strong desire by the *people themselves* to learn Irish. Never before have these summer courses been so crowded and never before has there been such demand from parents in large cities and towns for all-Irish schools. When the smog clears away from the Dublin civil service they may discover this change. Why is it our leaders are so lacking in vision that they see what is happening in the

## THE SECRET PLACES OF DONEGAL

here-and-now only when it is disappearing? Are they as dumb as military leaders who are always preparing for the last war?

The Horn Head peninsula is a place of wondrous beauty – a place of lonely, silent beaches, rocks that are 'His written word', caves where you might expect to see the fairies surfboarding on the backs of dolphins, and even leprechauns sitting on toadstools making golden slippers for the tripping sylphs. And the birds; there are thousands upon thousands of them, swirling, turning, swooping, diving. I sometimes envy them because they live in two worlds, the clear blue sky and the good rich earth. So do as I did, get out of your car and go for a long walk. You are on your holidays. You are not at a board-meeting or on a management course. Try to see things here with the mind of a child. Youth lives in the future, old age lives in the past, but the child lives in the present. And the present here in Donegal is beautiful. To the child everything is possible: fairies, goblins, giants, talking birds and animals. They can even see the angels, a joy denied to us adults. Poets like Francis Thompson wanted to be with children after death:

> And when, immortal mortal, droops your head
> And you, the child of deathless song, are dead;
> Then as you search with unaccustomed glance
> The ranks of Paradise for my countenance
> Among the learned counsellors of God;
> For if in Eden as on earth are we,
> I sure shall keep a younger company.

And the gifted author of *Alice in Wonderland* said:

> I'd give all the wealth, that toil hath piled
> The bitter fruit of life's decay
> To be once more a little child
> For one short summer day.

A word of warning however: beware of the leprechauns. You see, the leprechauns are partly human and for that reason they are thievish and dishonest. You might be well advised to leave your wallet behind just in case one of them offered to show you the three-card-trick. You would most surely come out the loser. However, you can be at your ease with all the others, even the animals. Not having any human element they can be trusted.

To the south is the much publicised Glenveagh National Park. When I presented myself at the entrance I was refused admission because I had Misty on a lead with me. 'No dogs allowed', I was told. It was high summer and I had the choice of leaving the little creature in the sweltering heat of the car, or of not going in. I chose the latter. I refuse on principle to inflict suffering on a helpless creature of God in order to satisfy an arbitrary regulation. I can understand why dogs should not be allowed to run free, but a dog controlled on a lead is surely a different matter. It is really a great pity that such an excellent unit as the National Parks and Monuments Service, who have done so much to improve Irish amenities, should support such silly rules. How much wiser it would be if they were to adopt a policy of giving maximum freedom to the public to enjoy themselves subject, however, to heavy fines if necessary, for any damage done. I did not, therefore, get to see Glenveagh National Park so I cannot write about it.

However I cannot resist the temptation to quote Professor Kingsley Porter who once owned Glenveagh House and park:

Never have there been so many laws nor so many unreasonable laws and never have laws been so rigorously enforced and so supinely obeyed. . .

It is a constant source of wonderment to me how the

# THE SECRET PLACES OF DONEGAL

*Lord Leitrim*

landlords of Donegal could live in surroundings of such extraordinary beauty and at the same time be so cruel. I would have thought that the glory of spring, the magic of summer, the mellowness of autumn and the wildness of winter, in such a magnificent environment as Glenveagh would have softened even the hardest heart. But it was not so. Even today there is an air of tragedy and sadness about this whole countryside as if the pain and sufferings inflicted by two brutal landlords, Lord Leitrim and George Adair, still lingered on like winter mists on the mountain peaks.

Leitrim was cantankerous, quarrelsome bully who evicted people on the slightest pretext, and in mid-winter flung women and little children out on the roadside to starve and die. He once evicted an educated and cultured hedge-schoolmaster because the schoolmaster in a moment of temper said to him, 'You may think you are a great man because you have a title but when you go to hell Dante won't even condescend to piss on you.'

He seems to have had over-active sexual glands and he demanded full satisfaction from all his tenants' daughters night or day, wet or fine as the mood took him. If they refused then the whole family faced eviction. With this threat hanging over them the parents were so terrified that they vied with each other in offering him their daughters. But the day came when he came face to face with justice. In April 1878 when he was returning from Lifford court, where he had got more eviction orders, he was ambushed and shot dead. His executioners escaped and, despite the offer of massive rewards, were never brought to trial. For a long time afterwards the Irish people drank the health of his killers with the following toast:

> Here's to the hand that made the ball
> That shot Lord Leitrim in Donegal.

In a County Donegal pub over a few pints an old man who told me he was a descendant of one of the evicted families, drank to that very toast and gave me an interesting if somewhat Rabelaisian account of his Lordship:

'I think what was wrong with Lord Leitrim was he had a troublesome little piece of machinery, and he had to have a tenant's daughter, or maybe two, every day of his life to satisfy it. 'Tis said that some of the tenants' houses he built had no back door so that the daughter couldn't escape when His Lordship arrived with a notion. I heard me grandfather telling about one tenant who was saving a bit of hay with his wife and daughter when Lord Leitrim arrived on his horse. He dismounted and demanded immediate attention from the daughter. As they were getting down to business on the headland the father was so terrified that he whispered to the daughter to keep her rump well up so that His Lordship would not be discommoded by the nettles. The poor man was right for don't you see if His Lordship's jewellery got stung there'd be hell to pay. They might even get evicted. That's the kind of a man he was, the Lord have mercy on him. All the same they didn't have to kill him. 'Twas said at the time that on account of his little problem he hadn't too long to live. Don't you know 'tis how the poor man spent the whole of his life digging his own grave with you-know-what. But I suppose that's the way with the world. There's some who have a lot of trouble with it and others don't have enough trouble at all. You can't satisfy everybody and if you don't boil the cabbage you can't ate it and if you boil it too much 'tis only fit for pigs. 'Tis all in the hands of God.'

Lord Leitrim was succeeded by his nephew, a decent honourable man who treated his tenants in a fair and just way and to some extent made amends for the barbarity of his uncle.

*George Adair*

George Adair was an entirely different kettle of fish. He does not seem to have had the little problem that tantalised Lord Leitrim, but on balance he may have been worse. He was a cunning, ruthless land speculator who trampled on the rights of everyone in the pursuit of financial gain.

After he purchased the Glenveagh estates he decided to turn them into huge sheep farms and to do so he had to get rid of most of the tenants. But he needed a good excuse and his cunning was not found wanting. He decided to goad them to breaking point and he instructed his chief steward, James Murray, a man with a criminal background, to lean heavily and harass the tenants as much as possible. In this way Murray made himself so obnoxious that he was hated and detested by the tenants. Then one November morning he went up the mountain

## GWEEDORE – GARTAN

with his dog to check on some sheep. He did not return that evening, but his dog, stained with blood, did. Two days later a search party found his dead body. His head had been battered in. His killers were never found.

This gave Adair the excuse he wanted. He publicly blamed his tenants for killing Murray and he evicted 50 families comprising 250 men, women and children. He levelled 28 houses to the ground. The eviction scenes in themselves were harrowing. One old man who had built his house stone by stone and reared his family kissed each wall before it was flattened to the ground. A poor widow and her seven children threw themselves on the ground and their crying resounded through the mountains as their little home was levelled to the ground. In another house a bedridden old man was carried out in his bed while the house was being knocked. The desolation all around was beyond description.

*The Londonderry Standard* reported:

When dispossessed the families grouped themselves on the ground beside their late home. . . As night set in the scene became fearfully sad. Passing along the base of the mountain the spectator might have observed near to each house its former inmates crouching round a turf fire close by a hedge; and as the rain poured upon them they found no cover. Many of them were miserably clad and on all sides the greatest desolation was apparent. . . These poor starving people remain on the cold bleak mountain, no one caring for them, whether they live or die. It's horrible to think of, but more horrible to behold.

John George Adair had won and from the luxury and opulance of Glenveagh Castle he celebrated his victory over the Irish peasant. The estates became the vast sheep farm he desired.

Yet in subsequent years there were a lot of strange murmerings, even among his own class. It was widely believed that the tenants did not kill Murray but that Adair himself planned it and paid a handsome sum to have it carried out. Dugdale Rankin, another employee of Adair's, who was a lodger in the Murray house, was having an affair with Murray's wife and local belief was that Adair paid him to murder Murray, thus giving him the excuse to blame the tenants. A local report states tersely and laconically that immediately after the funeral Rankin 'moved into Mrs Murray's bed.'

Before Adair died he had a monument erected to commemorate his memory. It was a huge boulder overlooking the lake with the inscription: 'John Adair, just, generous and true.' Shortly after the work was completed it was struck by lightning and broken to bits.

Adair escaped an Irish bullet by dying in America. His body was brought back and buried in his native Leix. Beside Adair's grave is another grave, that of Edward Mead who wrote a book called *The Dastard's Guide to Fame and Fortune*. They should have much in common to discuss with one another.

The shattered remains of many of these little homes are still to be seen around and about Glenveagh. Stop your car, pause for a few minutes and go into one of them. Sit down on a stone outside the door and transport yourself back one hundred years. Imagine that it was you who built this little home, stone by stone, plank by plank; that you brought your beautiful young bride here full of the joy of boundless love; that you began your married life here, brought children into the world, paid your rent and worked twelve or fourteen hours a day just to rear your family and barely keep alive; then one day you and your family are evicted, the home that you built crowbarred to the ground; Hear the cries and lamentations of your wife and children – your children – then perhaps you may get some idea of the horror and savagery of it all. And it did not happen only in Glenveagh. It happened in every village and townland in Ireland. This little visualisation may help you to understand the feelings of the Irish people towards the British Establishment, even after 100 years. As the old Irish proverb puts it: *It's easy to sleep on another man's wound.*

*George Russell*

Later Glenveagh was bought by Kingsley Porter who died so mysteriously off Inishbofin. His friend George Russell (AE) stayed at a little summer cottage in the woods nearby and he was a regular guest of the Porter's at Glenveagh Castle. AE was a brilliant conversationalist and Lucy Porter recalls her friends sitting around in the drawing room listening thoughtfully as he ranged over almost every conceivable subject. He was really a mystic who would seem much more at home in a Himalayan ashram than in a suburban house in Rathgar where he lived. He was a very good poet, overshadowed of course by Yeats. They were close friends and constant companions until in the end, as so often happens, they bored each other to tears. I suppose a point is reached in every companionship where two people have nothing to say to each other.

AE was an interesting example of that type of man who was a very good Irishman but who had some strange hankering after the British. Yeats too was like that and he would have accepted a knighthood from the crown when it was offered to him but Maude Gonne MacBride stopped him. AE was a pacifist, but he was also a realist and there is one telling comment of his which might be studied carefully by Irish politicians today. 'Although I have always condemned violence,' he said, 'we got nothing in Ireland by peaceful means. Yes, all the freedom the Irish have attained has been by fighting, violence and bloodshed.'

He was completely opposed to the 1916 Rising, yet, unlike so many others he could not bring himself to condemn it:

> Their dream had left me numb and cold
>   But yet my spirit rose in pride
> Refashioning in burnished gold
>   The images of those who died
> Or men shut in the penal cell.
> Here's to you, Pearse, your dream not mine
>   But yet the thought for this you fell
> Has turned life's water into wine.
>
> I listened to high talk from you
>   Thomas MacDonagh, and it seemed
> The words were idle, but they grew
>   To nobleness by death redeemed
> Life cannot utter words more great
>   Than life may meet by sacrifice

## GWEEDORE – GARTAN

> High words were equalled by high fate
> You paid the price! You paid the price!

He spent his holidays for thirty years in Donegal. When he was asked why he did not go abroad or go somewhere else he whimsically replied that he had not yet seen all of Donegal.

But a day came when the shadow of death approached and he had to say 'goodbye' to Donegal for the last time. He penned these words:

> I look on wood and hill and sky
>   Yet without any tears
> To the warm earth I bid 'goodbye'
>   For what unnumbered years.
>
> So many times my spirit went
>   This dark transfiguring way
> Nor ever knew what dying meant
>   Deep night or a new day.
>
> So many times it went and came
>   Deeper than thought it knows
> Unto what majesty of flames
>   In what wide heaven it goes.

When he died Ireland lost one of its noblest souls.

There is another secret place in Glenveagh – a place far from crowds, where, in beautiful historic surroundings, you can sit and meditate and let yourself slip back much more than a thousand years into the Ireland of long ago. It is near the back entrance to Glenveagh Park on the shores of a little lake called Lough Akibborn. It is called the Oratory of Colmcille. There you will see the ruins of a small church and what remains of an altar. This is supposed to have been the first church founded by St Colmcille. Inside the ruin there is what is known as the Natal Stone and tradition holds that it was on this stone that Colmcille was born. Why his mother should select a stone to endure her labour pains is not quite clear. Yet today it is a minor place of pilgrimage for pregnant women who either lie on the stone or kneel beside it and pray for an easy delivery.

I am one of those who advocate that St Colmcille should be our national saint. I have never been able to accept St Patrick as our national apostle. He was a Roman and he thought like a Roman, that is in straight lines. He was much more an administrator than an apostle – the French have a very descriptive word for it: *functionaire*. St Patrick did not really convert the Irish to Catholicism – large sections of them were already converted. What he did do was to try and organise the church into units obedient to Rome. And the poor man certainly had his work cut out for him dealing with the mercurial Celts. The early church in Ireland tended to ignore Rome, thumb their noses at the pope and go their own way. Patrick put in train a system of organisation that would reverse this situation but it was to take seven centuries before it succeeded. That happened in 1155 when Pope Adrian IV 'granted and donated Ireland' to the English King, Henry II 'to be held by him and his successors'. Since then Rome has always recognised Britain's right to dominate and rule Ireland and this policy was reinforced even by the present Pope John Paul II and indeed can be seen in operation today in the six counties where a majority of the ecclesiastics are backing the British. As the late Mgr Ronald Knox said: 'He who travels in the barque of Peter had better not look too close into the engine room.'

But Colmcille was in a different category altogether. He was an Irishman through and through, and possessed those rare Irish qualities of leadership which characterised our great leaders like Brian Boru and Michael Collins – patriotism, organisational ability, political sensitivity and the ruthlessness to carry through his decisions. Even if he only founded half the churches and monasteries attributed to him that would still be a great achievement in any one lifetime.

The reason for his exile to Iona are still not clear but it does look as if it were self-imposed and a plausible reason might well be remorse for those whose deaths he caused in battle. For a man who loved Ireland so much it was an extremely painful decision. When I was a schoolboy I learned a little poem the words of which were put into the mouth of Colmcille. I do not know who the talented author was and I can only remember two verses, but even those two catch the deep sense of tragedy. Colmcille and his companions had reached Orsenay in Scotland and they were going to settle there but when they climbed the cliffs they could see the shores of Ireland in the distance, so they had to move and find a place from where they could not see their native land:

> To oars again we may not stay
> For on the ocean's rim I see
> From the high cliffs of Orsenay
> The isle so dear to me.
>
> Far from Derry, far from Kells,
> And fair Raphoe my steps must be
> The psalms of Durrow's quiet dells
> The tone of Aran's holy bells
> Will sound no more for me.

Colmcille's long life and achievements on Iona are well known. After this rich and fulfilling mission he died on 9 June 597. He was not ill in any way and his death was not sudden. It was a soft tender summer's evening. The sea lapped gently on the shore. Every little eddy seemed to speak of peace. The monastery gardens were a blaze of colour. There was a faint delicate smell of new-mown hay. In the distance birds sang their evening vespers. He wandered slowly around the monastery, pausing here and there as if he were saying 'goodbye'. He then turned his face towards his Donegal homeland and stood in silent thought for a long time.

He seemed to have had a clear premonition of his death as happens with so many of the spiritually great in this world. He was seventy-six years of age – more than the biblical three score and ten – an old man, tired, weary and exhausted. As he stood there gazing across towards Donegal his old white horse limped slowly up to him. He began to whine mournfully and plaintively and to caress Colmcille's bosom with his head. He too seems to have known what was hidden from human beings, that his master was about to die.

Colmcille returned reflectively to his cell and continued his work of transcribing the Old Testament. For no apparent reason he stopped in the middle of a sentence and rested. When the bell rang for midnight prayers he rushed to the church and collapsed in front of the altar. Surrounded by his monks and lying in the arms of one, Diarmaid, the old man died. It is recorded that his face had the countenance of a youth.

Like Colmcille the monks of Ireland's past did not fear death. For them death was not the end but the beginning. They believed that at the moment of death every human being was given a last chance to decide his destiny. Throughout their lives, they reasoned, their powers of knowing were heavily restricted by the limitations of human nature, and because of these crippling restrictions they could not know God fully. Blinded by earthly pressures they only got glimpses of him. Again, they reasoned that if they did not know him fully they could not make a total choice for or against him. But at the moment of death all these chains are burst and the free illuminating power of knowledge and perception of their divine nature is realised. At that moment and that moment only, they believed, could they make a final choice.

But that final choice would be heavily conditioned by the kind of life they lived. If divine nature were the predominant driving force of their lives then their choice would be for God. If on the other hand their human nature was the predominant force then their choice might well be against him. It is not too hard to see what the life force in men and women of Colmcille's calibre was, and so they looked forward to death as the real source of life in much the same way as young lovers look forward to their wedding-day.

Death is a subject which holds an unending fascination for most people and I plead guilty to this myself. I am a haunter of graveyards and there are few places one can contemplate it as well as here in Colmcille's Oratory in Gartan. Here you can meet up with the great reality that you must one day die and unless you have reached the point where the divine element in your life is in charge this can be a sobering and even frightening thought. When we sing, drink and carouse death is merely asleep under the table. Even the very headstones in a graveyard give out their warning:

*Hodi mihi, Cras tibi! Today for me, tomorrow for you!*

>   Observe the dew-drenched rose of Tyrian grain
>   A rose today. But will you ask in vain
>   Tomorrow what it is; and yesterday
>   It was the dust, the sunshine and the rain.

If death were only a probability one could understand our lust for pleasure, but death is certain. How then can we be so joyful and sometimes so happy if we live in the shadow of this merciless Reaper? Most probably because we know in the very depths of our being that we are immortal and that we never really die.

If we believe, as I do, that the majority of people make the right choice at the moment of death then a graveyard takes on a more pleasant aspect. It is no longer a place of gloom, sorrow or sadness, but almost a place of envy, where all suffering ends and eternal joy begins. The dead are free from the pains and sufferings of this life. They exist in one complete act of perpetual love. Their intellects are so powerful that they see all the mysteries of life in one vision. They know the answers to every question that ever baffled the human mind. They know the last revealing chapter in the mysterious book of life. They are so far superior to us in beauty, love and happiness as to defy understanding by an imperfect human brain. It is they who must surely pity us.

But a graveyard should serve as a gentle warning too. A warning that beyond the grave there are no popes or cardinals, no kings or queens, no lords or dukes, no decorations or medals, no TV presenters and above all no money. The dead face their new world holding in their hands only what they *were* in this life, not what they *had*, only their unselfishness, their generosity and their love – above all their love. For love is the only thing in life that seems to be able to rise above death. In one of his most beautiful poems Maurice Baring puts death in the perspective of a person in love:

## GWEEDORE – GARTAN

I watched you and I knew that I had found
The long-delaying, long-expected spring
I knew my heart had found a time to sing;
The strength to soar was in my spirit's wing
That life was full of a triumphant sound
That death could only be a little thing.

There I go again! Always scribbling about death! I apologise!

## FOUR

# GARTAN – FANAD – DROMBOE

> *It is not in the song*
> *The sadness is*
> *But in the thoughts that throng*
> *Remembrances*
>                     TERENCE MacSWINEY

The great peninsulas of County Donegal – Fanad, Rossguill and Inishowen range out towards the north as if they were defying the wild seas of the Atlantic. They enclose hundreds of sheltered, land-locked bays that are a delight to the lovers of boating as they are to the tourist in search of peace.

The wonderful drive from Portnablagh through Ards, Creeslough, Carrigart, Downings, Doagh and along Mulroy Bay to Milford is one of unsurpassed beauty and is exceptionally well described in all the tourist literature.

If you study the guide-books carefully you will find scores of little places where you can sit and enjoy the silence and stillness of nature. Stillness can bring us into very close touch with our surroundings in such a way that the beauty of those surroundings seems to become part of us. The body can become part of the rocks and moorland; the soul can soar higher and glide from peak to peak.

Or if you sit quietly by the sea the air around you can become permeated by loveliness. As the tide goes out sorrow can go with it and as it comes in slowly it can bring serenity. Indeed a different self can come into being – a more beautiful self than you ever guessed existed.

Along this route is another of my secret places of Donegal. It is Ards Monastery, or Ard Mhuire as it is known locally. It is now a place of retreat run by that great religious order the Capuchin Fathers, but in the last century it was the home of a British planter named Stewart who was one of the most brutal and savage landlords ever to be inflicted on the people of Donegal. In the bad days of the land war it is alleged he left a trail of blood, murder, rape and destruction behind him which caused Michael Davitt to write:

> On highways side
>   Where oft were seen
> The wild dog and the vulture keen
>   Tug for the limbs
> And gnaw the face
>   Of some starved child
> Of our Irish race.

It is strange to think that here in this haven of beauty, where so much evil and depravity were once contrived, there is now a house of goodness, prayer and love. A cancerous running sore has been replaced by a sparkling jewel of rare beauty – that is how the angels in the sky see it, a young teenager with a mini-skirt told me.

Since they came to Ireland five hundred years ago, the Capuchins have never ceased to serve the Irish people, particularly the poor, the weak and the downtrodden.

## THE SECRET PLACES OF DONEGAL

When so many other ecclesiastics were compromising with our rulers in return for tinsel, the Capuchins stood out head and shoulders in their fidelity to Irish ideals. They never abandoned their belief in the right of all Ireland to complete freedom and many of them suffered severely in consequence. Few realise what terrible pressures were brought to bear on them by a hierarchy which was almost totally pro-British. Such was the outlook of the Irish bishops at one period that they compelled the students and staff at Maynooth to take the following oath:

I . . . do take almighty God and his only son Jesus Christ my Redeemer to witness that I will be faithful and bear true allegiance to our most gracious sovereign lord King George the Third and him will defend to the utmost of my power against all conspiracies and attempts whatever that shall be made against his person, crown and dignity; and I will do my utmost endeavour to disclose and make known to his Majesty and his heirs all treasons and traitorous conspiracies which may be formed against him or them: and I do faithfully promise to maintain, support and defend to the utmost of my power the succession of the crown in his Majesty's family against any person or persons.

I cannot but feel ashamed of the role of my church played over the centuries. As an official body they stood full square behind the British but their perfidy is made somewhat easier to forgive when one thinks of some of the wonderful individual priests who took Christ's teaching literally and who threw their lot in with the poor starving Irish. Within the Irish church one can distinguish two minds: the ecclesiastical mind and the spiritual mind. The latter is in the minority.

The Capuchins took no such oath as was taken in Maynooth. Their history sparkles with the names of great and outstanding men. Unfortunately for me I got to know only two of these priests well.

The first was Father James O'Mahony, professor of philosophy at University College, Cork. James had one of the most brilliant minds I ever encountered in a human being. As well as holding degrees in philosophy and literature he held an Agregé from the University of Louvain, a degree so rare and so difficult to obtain that at the time only three people in Europe held it. During the war years when I was a young lieutenant in Cork I cycled once a week to his monastery on the western outskirts of the city where, over a cup of tea, he initiated me into the secrets of philosophy. There were few subjects in the realms of the spirit that were not threshed out in those discussions and all my life I carried with me some of the maxims he gave me:

'When the wise man points towards the sun the fool sees only the finger.'

'Happiness is not an entity it is only a by-product of life.'

'Depression is only frozen anger.'

'There is nothing whatever wrong with getting the most out of life if we give the most to life.'

'Mental laziness is the biggest obstacle to union with God.'

'Everyman is alone in what he knows about the wreckage of himself.'

'Take our cultural background away from us and something in us dies.'

It was he who influenced me to give up a safe secure professional job in the army to enter the hazardous world of books where the casualties are the highest of any profession. 'You cannot waste your life doing nothing,' he said. 'Water that does not flow stagnates.' Despite enormous difficulties and problems I have never regretted that decision. It was one which brought me a life of great purpose and fulfilment.

# THE SECRET PLACES OF DONEGAL

Despite the variety of our wide-ranging discussions we returned again and again to one topic: death. (Yes, you guessed right!) What happens when we die? What is the spirit like? What is the other world like? What is God like? This latter question he used to answer facetiously himself: 'First of all she is black. . .

One evening when I called he was in a particularly playful mood. 'At last,' he said, with a twinkle in his eye, 'I know what happens after death.'

'What?' I queried.

'I was visiting a convent today and a holy nun told me that after the Resurrection we will get our bodies back *but only from the top of the chest up* and,' he added, 'she really believed it.'

Then came a day when I gazed down at his dead body in a coffin. I was filled with conflicting emotions but one thought kept haunting my mind: 'Now you know the answer. Now you have read the last chapter in the book of life. Now you are at one with whatever is out there; and I am still here, confused.'

The second great Capuchin to honour me with friendship was Father Aloysius Travers. Aloysius was an altogether different personality from James. I doubt if he ever read a philosophic book since his student days and I am quite sure he would be horrified if he heard James referring to God, however humorously, as a negress. He had no problems about what happened after death. His faith provided the straightforward answer. Aloysius was a pastoral priest totally committed to the care of souls and in that work he excelled. As I got to know him better he spoke to me of his experiences during the 1916 rising.

James Connolly lying wounded in hospital and surrounded by British soldiers, sent for him and said: 'It is as a priest I want to see you. I have seen and heard of the brave conduct of the priests and nuns during the week. I believe they are the best friends of the workers.' This telling sentence is somewhat of an embarrassment to the highly paid anti-clerical socialist politicians of today. Aloysius then heard Connolly's confession and gave him Holy Communion. Because of his wounds Connolly could not stand so he was strapped to a chair, taken to the gloomy yard of Kilmainham Jail and shot.

Both Pádraig Pearse and Thomas MacDonagh sent for Aloysius and he heard their confessions and gave them Holy Communion in Kilmainham Jail. Then they walked bravely to face the British firing squad. Both of them told Aloysius that they were in no way afraid and that they did not know how they deserved the great honour of dying for Ireland.

Aloysius heard old Tom Clarke's confession. Clarke, who had spent eighteen years in British jails, was allowed one hour with his wife in the cell before he was shot. All the while, however, a British soldier was present holding a stump of a candle in a jam-pot.

Conditions in the jail were made appalling for the leaders. There was no light in any of the cells and the condemned men had to sit in the dark and contemplate their fate. No toilet facilities were available other than a dirty bucket which the prisoners could empty once a day. No toilet paper was provided.

If ever you get a chance do visit the gloomy cells in Kilmainham from where these brave men walked to their deaths. You can follow their footsteps into the dark claustrophobic execution yard where they fell to British bullets. Just across the road from the jail is the Royal Hospital, Kilmainham. This was turned into the headquarters of the British army which crushed the rising and planned the executions. You will probably find it hard to understand, as I do, why an Irish government, made possible by Pearse and Connolly, would spend twenty million pounds restoring these royal buildings and commemorating the soldiers who smashed the Rising. You will probably wonder too, when, if ever, will we stop genuflecting and get up off our knees.

Today, not just in Ireland, but all over the world 11,000 Capuchins translate the ideals of their founder, the gentle St Francis, into reality. Their lifestyle is one of kindness, understanding and love. Their monasteries extend the hand of welcome and friendship to all comers. Nowhere is this more evident than here at graceful picturesque Ards. The beautiful grounds have been thrown open to the public. Here retreats of spiritual renewal are regularly conducted and where better can one go to turn inwards and penetrate the depths of one's own soul, examine the mistakes and sorrows of one's life, than here in the tranquil serene surroundings of Ard Mhuire. Over the last ten years some 18,000 lay people and 2,000 priests have sought to 'make their souls', as the old Donegal phrase goes, here.

Not too far away from Ards Monastery, near Creeslough, is another secret place of Donegal, Doe Castle, described by Gerald Griffin:

> Peaceful it stands, the mighty pile
> By many a heart's blood once defended
> Yet silent now as cloistered aisle
> Where rung the sounds of banquet splendid.

But the history of Doe castle was anything but a peaceful one. It was the home of the MacSweeney clan, regretfully nicknamed MacSweeney of the Battleaxe. They were a violent tempestuous family – one of them hung seven workmen for turning up late – for whom murder or treachery held little scruple. It was to here that Inghean Dubh O'Donnell sent her teenage son Red Hugh to be trained in all the arts: literature, music, swordmanship, endurance, horesemanship and such other educational pursuits as befitted a young Irish prince.

There is some kind of magic about the personality of Red Hugh that seems to have survived the centuries, and one can feel this strange nostalgic magic walking around the fields and woods and shores where he trained and rode and hunted and, I suppose, wenched like so many other young Irish princes of his lineage. Here he was to learn the strategy and tactics that he later used so often and so successfully against the British.

Red Hugh is one of those youths who has captured the imagination of the Irish people in the same way as the young Finn MacCumhail, Cuchulain, and in modern times Kevin Barry and Bobby Sands. Biographers have been at pains to try to explain the magical quality they had which so endeared them to the public. It is something that is very hard to define but more than anything else it must be the idealism they lived and their readiness to give up their young lives for those ideals. The world always bows its head before the man it cannot break.

All the world too, they say, loves a lover and Doe Castle has its own Romeo and Juliet story. Turlough O'Boyle, a young farmer of beauty and strength fell in love with Aileen, daughter of Maolmhuire MacSweeney of Doe Castle. His love was returned but old Maolmhuire was not having any of this romance for his beloved daughter. He wanted a much better match for her and when she refused to give Turlough up, he had him discreetly strangled one wild stormy night in the castle dungeons. Aileen saw the murderers trying to dispose of the body and when she realised who it was she jumped from the battlements to her death. The gifted Creeslough poet Niall Mac Giolla Bhride tells what happened:

Then with a shriek she madly jumped from the tower to the ground
Where by her faithful waiting-maid her gory corpse was found
And in the Castle graveyard green beneath the mouldering soil
Maolmhuire's daughter sleeps in death with Turlough Óg O'Boyle

And fishers say along the beach a phantom boat is seen
To gently glide by pale moonlight adown by Lackagh stream
While in that boat two figures float, and on each face a smile
They say it is young Aileen and her Turlough Óg O'Boyle.

*Misty*

## GARTAN – FANAD – DRUMBOE

So if you care to come back to the Castle some moonlight night maybe you'd see the two lovers gently gliding in their little boat over the still waters, but be careful you do not disturb them because they know that the spell of everlasting love can be destroyed by the presence of other human beings.

One of the unusual things about Doe Castle is the vibes it gives off. Unlike Leamenagh Castle in the Burren which smells of evil, Doe is a mixture of good and evil. Maybe this is because of the influence of the nearby graveyard and monastic ruins. This little burial ground is truly a haven of peace. Hundreds, if not thousands of bodies have been buried here – saints and sinners, warriors and monks, wise men and fools. For them the strife is over and they are all now together in the great companionship of death. The silence and tranquillity of so many nameless graves seem to cry out and say: 'What was it all about? Was it ever worth it? We are now only dust and clay and Doe Castle is the possession of jackdaws and crows.'

The Fanad peninsula is one of extraordinary beauty which blends together rolling picturesque countryside with indented, weather-beaten coasts. It begins at Milford where the modern Catholic church is well worth a visit. It is a church that is not only artistic but prayerful as well. A church is primarily a house of prayer and its art should respond to the deepest yearnings of its people and not to the divergent opinions of any school of artists. Here in Milford everything about it is intelligible to the people whom it was built to serve.

The road from Milford to Kerrykeel runs along the shores of Mulroy bay where, according to tradition, the fish are very scarce on account of some little altercation with Saint Colmcille some time back. An old fisherman told me what happened:

'Poor Colmcille, God rest his soul, suffered from an embarrassing little ailment called piles, and in them days there was no proper ointment. The cure was a mixture of sand and seaweed taken from the in-coming tide. Well anyway, he was attending to this little matter one fine day on the shores of Mulroy Bay when a fishin' boat landed near him. He pulled up his corduroys as quick as he could and pretended to be looking for scallops. When he came up to the fishermen he asked them for a few fish but they refused to give him any. You see they thought he was a tramp from Cork by the cut of him! If they knew he was Colmcille they'd have given him the full of the boat. Anyway he put the curse of Cromwell on themselves and on Mulroy Bay and that's why the fishin' was always bad ever since.'

I find it a sheer delight to listen to such stories told by ordinary country people. They may not be strictly accurate but then it is a well known principle of Irish pub-talk that one does not let accuracy get in the way of a good story. But I am especially intrigued by their sense of familiarity with the past, and how they treat a thousand years as if it were only yesterday. Colmcille was as real to this man as his next-door neighbour. He was not someone with a halo or someone living up in the clouds in the odour of sanctity. He was an ordinary man irritated by a little ailment that can beset any human being. He was one of the people – that is how it should be and that of course is what Christ was.

I remember a Clareman telling me what a fine looking man Brian Boru was. He wore the tallest hat going to mass on Sunday, he said. Another local near Clonmacnoise discussed Dervogilla's little weakness for the men as if he was talking about a neighbour's daughter. Her mother brought her up too strictly, he said. She made her go to Mass and

## GARTAN – FANAD – DRUMBOE

Communion every day and 'tis said that she had to tie her legs together with the brown scapular every time a man came to the house. Of course when she got free of her mother she went wild altogether. I can tell you, he concluded, she wasn't long getting rid of the scapulars then. She had so many lovers that they had to bury her in a Y-shaped coffin when she died.

That either daily mass or the scapular or coffins did not come into being until hundreds of years after Dervogilla's death was only a minor detail, and it would be the height of bad manners to comment on it. It would seem that one was bragging about one's superior knowledge – and there is no way you will get put into place as surely as if you try to show yourself superior. Anyway you're not superior! The countryman is giving expression to a culture with thousands of years behind it while you are most likely regurgitating the empty view of some plastic television presenter. When you're listening to a good story don't allow yourself to be carried away by historical accuracy. 'All history is bunk,' exclaimed Henry Ford and if you read some of the modern Irish historians you may well be inclined to agree with him.

One of the few things that can annoy me in my old age is when people ask me if the stories I told in my books were really true. I recorded them as I heard them and I never insulted any teller by questioning the accuracy of what he had to say. If I have misled my readers then I have been misled myself. To those who are ardently searching for truth perhaps a travel book is not the best source. I would recommend the *Summa Theologica* by St Thomas Aquinas in twenty volumes. I believe it can be bought on the hire purchase, and if that does not suit there is always the Penny Catechism.

# THE SECRET PLACES OF DONEGAL

The trip up to Fanad Head and back along the shores of Lough Swilly is one of extraordinary beauty. The view from Knockalla mountain near Ballymacstocker Bay is simply superb. Up along the north Fanad coast there are extraordinary rock formations – The Seven Arches, The Great Arch and many others. All this area is well described in the guide books and tourist literature and while it is a recognised route there are scores of little secret places where you can pause and contemplate in perfect peace.

Look out for one of these secret places near Fanad Head. It is in a small field a short distance west of Arryherra Cross. Here you will see some standings stones but they are not archaeological remains. They mark the graves of unknown persons, men, women and children whose bodies were washed ashore at different times. Who are they? How did they come to die in the sea? Shipwreck? Suicide? Accident? We do not know. They brought their secret to the grave. Their epitaph might well be that inscribed on the tomb of the Unknown Soldier: *Known only to God*. Do bend your knee and remember them in prayer. Few others will do so.

If at all possible spend a few days here in the Fanad peninsula. It is a fairyland of beauty where you have everything you want at hand; secret places to contemplate alone; not so secret places where you can socialise and enjoy yourself; and the people of Fanad are a sheer delight to converse with.

It was in this general area in a pleasant hostelry, where exactly I shall not say, a little adventure befell me that looks as if it came straight out of the pages of Balzac, Maupassant or O. Henry. It was one of those pranks that turned horribly sour. A young friend of mine, a beautiful girl half my age, decided out of the goodness of her heart that I should have a rest and she drove me around for a whole day. We called to this hostelry to quench our thirst and there we fell into conversation with a couple in their late thirties who were holidaying in Donegal. I was dressed in a light fawn summer suit with a jet black polo-necked jumper. As the drinks loosened our tongues and we became more friendly the lady looked rather quizzically at me and said; 'I have a strange feeling that you are a priest. Am I right?'

'You are indeed,' I lied, 'and the young girl here is a nun. We are having a little holiday together in Donegal.'

I must have looked rather appealingly at her because she said in a low voice: 'Of course I understand. I fully understand.'

There was an ever so slight emphasis on the word 'fully'. After half an hour or so of pleasant drinking and sparkling conversation we had to leave. The lady walked to the hall with us and then rather suddenly turned to me and asked if she could have a word with me alone. My young companion continued on to the car and in a low voice the lady said to me: 'I think you are an understanding kind of priest. Is there any chance you would hear my confession? You see, I am a nun and my companion is an old boyfriend of my youth who is now married with a young family.'

For a few awful moments I was tempted. I would have dearly loved to hear her story but I quickly came to my senses and saw it would be too much. It would be going too far with the farce.

'I'm sorry,' I said, 'I have no faculties for this diocese. The whole thing would be invalid.'

'Pity,' she said sadly. 'A great pity.'

At that moment I felt a certain mute contempt for myself, and then one of those extraordinary flashes from somewhere in outer space came to me and almost without knowing it I heard myself saying: 'Whatever you do don't break up a marriage and destroy the lives of innocent children. You'll never forgive yourself for it. But do enjoy to the full your little holiday in Donegal together and then say "goodbye". Someone long ago said: "If your sins are as red as scarlet I can make them as white as snow".'

I thought I saw a tear coming to her eye. Quietly and dignified she said softly: 'Thank you. Thank you ever so much.' Then she turned on her heel and went back into the pub. I never saw her again. Maybe it is better so.

It is well worth spending a day or even longer exploring the little town of Rathmullan on the Fanad peninsula. It is a charming old-world place where one meets history at every turn. Do purchase a small excellent pamphlet called *Rathmullan – A Walking Tour* by Margaret Carton and follow its directions. You will rarely enjoy a ramble as much.

It was here in Rathmullan that the young Red Hugh O'Donnell was kidnapped by the British and brought in chains to Dublin where he was to endure six years of the most appalling torture and suffering before he finally escaped. It happened this way:

In order to bring Donegal into subjection Sir John Perrot, the British gauleiter, decided they would have to destroy the O'Donnell armies. This however would take several thousand soldiers and he just did not have such a force at his disposal at that time. However he thought of another plan. 'Give me permission,' he said to his masters, 'to try a device I have in hand. I will quieten O'Donnell for you without the loss of one man. If my trick fails we can try force afterwards.' Perrot was given his head and he bribed a sea captain, appropriately enough named Skipper, to take fifty soldiers on board his ship and sail to Rathmullan with a cargo of white wine, pretending they came from Spain. Young Red Hugh, then only fifteen years of age, was staying at Rathmullan castle with the MacSweeneys, and he innocently went on board with a few friends to sample the wine. They were enjoying themselves in the captain's cabin when suddenly the British soldiers appeared, clapped them in irons and the ship set sail. They were to spend six long years living in terrible conditions mostly on food which they had to beg for through the prison bars.

This certainly had the effect of quieting the O'Donnells, who offered a ransom of £150,000 in today's money. Inghean Dubh, Red Hugh's mother, was harbouring twenty-five Spanish Armada survivors and she offered them in exchange for her son. This offer was accepted and the Spaniards were marched to Dublin to make the exchange. When the British got the Spaniards they beheaded them on the spot and refused to honour their agreement with Inghean Dubh. Why is it that we were, and are, the only country in the world to trust the word of a British politician?

Eventually after six agonising years Red Hugh made his escape but his treatment in prison filled him with a hatred of the British who were to pay dearly in lives for their inhuman cruelty over the ensuing years.

Near Rathmullan wood there is a little bay called Portnamurray and it was here that the last leaders of the Irish resistance, headed by the great Hugh O'Neill, left Ireland forever. It could be called the Irish Dunkirk, but unlike Dunkirk those who took flight were never to return. There were in all one hundred persons composed of the O'Neills, O'Donnells, MacSweeneys and other Irish leaders with their families and the group included that wonderful woman Nuala O'Donnell, who left her husband, Niall Garv, and cursed him because he was a traitor. Years later she was seen by the poet Mac an Bhaird mourning the last of her kinsmen at a Roman grave:

> O Woman of the piercing wail
> Who mourns o'er yon mound of clay

> With sigh and groan.
> Would God you were among the Gael
> You would not then from day to day
> Weep thus alone.
>
> Then, daughter of O'Donnell, dry
> Thine overflowing eyes, and turn
> Thy heart aside
> For Adam's race is born to die,
> And sternly the sepulchral urn
> Mocks human pride.

Should they have left Ireland or should they have stayed and fought? In retrospect it is easy to be wise. The old Irish proverb says: 'The hurler sitting on the ditch always knows best.' However I think there is a case to be made for the belief that the Flight was a mistake.

After the disaster at Kinsale one of the worst traits in the Irish character surfaced in most parts of the country. Many of the great Irish clans, believing the British to be the winners, threw their lot in with them in the hope of currying favour and holding on to their lands and properties. The British exploited this treachery to the full and within a year O'Neill found himself hemmed in on all sides with only a few hundred fighting men. British troops had devastated his lands and destroyed the crops. Famine was rife. There are recorded cases of starving children eating the corpses of their dead mothers. O'Donnell had gone to Spain to raise an army of 10,000 men, but the British, realising what a dangerous man he was, sent one of their agents named Blake to poison him. Some say he succeeded, others say that O'Donnell died of natural causes. The one thing that is certain is that he died. O'Donnell's death was a deadly blow to O'Neill. It was the straw that broke the camel's back. Old, weary and heartbroken he decided to give up and leave Ireland forever.

If O'Donnell had not gone to Spain, but remained behind things might have been different. He was an intelligent, able, ruthless soldier, who like Michael Collins in later years, fully grasped that the only language the British ever understood is that which comes from the barrel of a gun. Like Collins he would have been ruthless with the Irish who helped the English. He would have executed them one after another without mercy and in this way could have stemmed the tide of desertions, consolidated a large measure of unity, made life impossible for the British in Ulster to start with, and eventually throughout all Ireland.

But that was not to happen. Instead Ireland lay crushed and broken at the feet of the British. There followed a campaign of extermination of the Irish people that left the Nazi extermination of the Jews look like a Sunday School tea party. Over the next generations close on 10,000,000 men, women and children of the Irish race were sent to their deaths with unparalleled brutality. Unlike the Nazis, however, there were no Nuremberg trials to bring the perpetrators to justice.

Today, it is a moving experience to sit on the shore at Portnamurray, close your eyes and go back in time to that terrible day when the ship left Lough Swilly and brought with it the battered remnants of the hopes and aspirations of the Irish people who were to live as slaves in the fullest sense for the next three hundred years.

The town of Letterkenny is regarded by most Donegal people as the capital of the county but this is hotly disputed by the people of Lifford – a dispute which I, all the way from Cork, have no intention of entering. The dominating feature of Letterkenny is, of course, the magnificent St Eunan's cathedral which is well worth a visit. I was told in

# THE SECRET PLACES OF DONEGAL

a pub that there was never a saint called Eunan and that it was some drunken abbot with a weakness for poteen and a slight cast in his eye, who misread the word 'Adamanan' and though it was 'Eunan' and so christened the old monastic site. However, it does not really matter very much for one saint is just as good as another. Anyway the word 'saint' is a bit of a misnomer. Most of those called saint were never formally canonised, and a lot of them were far from being saints in the strict theological sense. In the old days the word 'saint' meant 'learned' and in Hebrew it meant 'teacher', so that effectively most of the hierarchy of the old Irish church were referred to as saints, even though many of them were first rate scoundrels. Anyway Eunan or Adamanan, it does not really matter so long as he was a good sound Donegal man.

Not too far from Letterkenny there is a quiet, lonely, secret place – so secret indeed that I have never seen a soul there. Beside the Catholic church in Stranorlar there is a cross erected to the memory of all Donegal men and women who died in the fight for freedom. Just to the left of this cross there is a small road leading to Drumboe wood and if you drive along this road for five minutes or so you will see flagpoles and another cross in a field on your right-hand side. On this spot one morning in March 1923 four young Irishmen were executed by a Free State army firing squad. 'Executed' is probably too refined a word to use for this act – 'judicial murder' would describe it more correctly. The four men were Charlie Daly, Seán Larkin, Daniel Enright and Tim O'Sullivan. They had supported De Valera and taken the Republican side in the civil war. They were captured in a Free State round-up near Errigal mountain. They were charged before a court-martial with possession of arms and ammunition, and for this offence they were sentenced to death.

GARTAN – FANAD – DRUMBOE

The execution was set for 7 a.m. and at 4 p.m. the previous evening they were formally told that they would be shot the following morning. They were not allowed to see any of their relatives. In the few hours left they wrote their last letters to their families. All the letters show a great serenity and courage in the face of death. Charlie Daly wrote to his mother:

A Mathair Dílis,

My last message to you and all at home is not to worry about my death. Forget all about its physical and wordly aspect and look at it only from the spiritual and religious point of view. I am now within a few short hours of death and writing to you with a perfect calmness. . .

I won't say much about wordly affairs – they look very insignificant now – except that I am leaving all of you some souvenir or other. My clothes and a few other things will be sent home. . .

My death is one of the trials God is sending to you. I am confident that all of you will bear it in the way from which you will derive most spiritual benefit. . . I can't imagine in what place, time or circumstances we could hope for a more favourable time to die. . .

I will say nothing about my life except that I hope it has been what a good Irishman's and Catholic's should have been. . .

I would like to write to all of you but since I won't have time I will say a prayer for them instead. The three other lads are splendid. Anyone looking in and seeing us writing letters would hardly believe that we will be with God in a couple of hours.

The same spirit of selflessness runs through the letters of his comrades. Their concern was for those they were leaving behind. Punctually at 7 a.m. they were blindfolded and shot.

This incident was only one of scores in the tragic civil war that followed the four glorious years of the freedom fight. The British fully achieved what they set out to do. Their old policy of 'divide and conquer' which had so brilliantly worked for hundred of years in Ireland was once more successful.

At the first commemoration of the deaths of the Drumboe martyrs the distinguished Donegal writer Seamus Ó Grianna said:

This time last year Drumboe was the scene of a terrible tragedy. Four young men were taken from their cells in the grey dawn of a March morning and their souls were hurled into eternity by a volley from a firing squad. . .

Tir Conaill is rich in historic spots, but Drumboe will be regarded in years to come as the greatest and holiest spot in the county – holier than Gartan's lakeside, greater than Donegal Abbey, more inspiring than the Rock of Doon – because while those places are associated with achievements attained when the tide of victory was with us, Drumboe is symbolic of one of those sacrifices which in the words of Terence MacSwiney, has the land unconquered and unconquerable.

These were brave and noble words but history was to prove them unprophetic. The ideals for which these young men gave their lives are now forgotten by Fiánna Fáil, the political party which arose to defend them. They are, however, very much alive in that great Donegal TD Neil Blaney, who never abandoned them. The Ireland these men died for does not exist today and it seems as if their sacrifices, and those of thousands of others, were in vain. As I write these lines in 1987 the Queen's writ now runs throughout Ireland and Mrs Thatcher seems to be our effective Taoiseach. When she cracks the whip most political knees in Ireland, including those of Fiánna Fáil, will genuflect.

The Anglo-Irish Agreement and the Extradition Act have shown that the British have out-witted and out-manoeuvred our politicians. Every single concession the British asked for, they got and they gave not one iota in return. Will the paramilitaries now retaliate by shooting Irish judges, politicians and civil servants? If so we might well have a civil war on our hands in the near future. Could it be that the British have manoeuvred us into this position knowing full well that a civil war would be the result? Every Irish politician to whom the destiny of the Irish people has been entrusted might usefully meditate carefully on the words of the late Lord Birkenhead: 'War by the Irish on the Irish is the kind of political development which I observe with great pleasure'.

As I wandered through the shadows of Drumboe wood that beautiful summer day I fell to considering again, even though I had done so often and often before, the nature of that strange institution known as the British Establishment; an institution that has sent millions of people to their deaths and that has so far escaped trial by any international court for their crimes.

The elaborate structure of British society is based on the principle that British interests are sacred and take precedence over every moral code. The unquestioning acceptance of this principle is indispensable to anyone wishing to hold any permanent place, however menial, in that powerful section of society known as the ruling class, that is politicians, civil servants, army and police officers, trade union officials, diplomats, judges, clergy, secret service agents, editors and newspaper owners, company directors and managers. Once total allegiance is given to these principles, then every pursuit, however unethical, degrading and untruthful, is permissible.

It is in perfect good taste to slaughter more than three hundred young sailors on the *Belgrano*, to cut the throats of Argentinian prisoners of war as they were captured, to murder children playing on the streets of Belfast with plastic bullets, to litter the six counties with thousands of graves, to slaughter thirteen thousand Kenyans whose only wish was that they might live as free people, to betray every trust, to double-cross friendly nations, to starve millions to death. All such things are permissible and indeed praiseworthy provided they are carried out by Her Majesty's servants, with Her Majesty's weapons and in Her Majesty's interest. The words 'Her Majesty' have an almost magical power to cover up realities. There is no such thing as Long Kesh Concentration Camp – there is only Her Majesty's Maze Prison. There is no such thing as Castlereagh Torture Centre – there is only Her Majesty's Castlereagh Police Barracks. There is no such thing as legalised terrorists whose trade is mainly murder. There is only Her Majesty's SAS. Like the whitened sepulchres of the scriptures, these magical words cover stupendous quantities of human bones.

It was to destroy that evil grip over Ireland that the young heroes died in Drumboe wood. It now looks as if they died in vain.

Perhaps the saddest thoughts of all that crowded my mind that day was when I recalled the frightening words of the great guerrilla leader, Tom Barry, spoken to Father McDyer:

We boast that we fought for seven hundred and fifty years until we finally got rid of them out of the twenty-six counties. I say that it is a shame that it took us so long and the reason is that we never united. Look at the rebellion of 1798. Most of the country stood by while there was such carnage at Vinegar Hill. Look at 1916 – there were many guns in Ireland then and if everyone had but fired a shot in the air they would have kept fresh contingents from assailing Dublin and extinguishing the fire of freedom in the GPO. I tell you, Father, don't worry too much about the EEC. *The Irish people are not worth fighting for* (italics mine).

# FIVE

# INNISHOWEN – AILEACH

> Yes, I must build it still, despite fools laughter
> I could not stay my hand. I would not try,
> Tho' all the dark of night shut down hereafter
> Should I now quench the star I follow by?
>
> TERENCE MacSWINEY

On the road from Letterkenny to the Inishowen peninsula there is a byroad two miles or so west of the village of Newtown-Cunningham which leads to the lonely rectory of Sharon, the scene of one of Donegal's most celebrated murders, or executions, depending on your point of view.

The victim was Dr William Hamilton, a Protestant clergyman from Fanad. The United Irishmen rebellion had just begun and Hamilton crossed by ferry from Fortstewart in Fanad to Ballybegley on the other shore of Lough Swilly. He then rode to Derry, laid information against a number of United Irishmen and arranged for a company of British troops to come from Derry to round them up the next day. This, of course, meant torture and almost certain death for the captives.

Because it was late evening and a storm had blown up he decided to stay overnight at Sharon Rectory with his friends Dr and Mrs Waller. It seems the Irish spies knew of his business in Derry and had him shadowed to the rectory. After a short while the place was surrounded by a body of armed men who demanded of the Wallers that they hand up what they called 'the bloodthirsty Hamilton'. Hamilton rushed into hiding in a cupboard under the stairs and the insurgents fired injuring Mrs Waller fatally. When they threatened to burn the house and its occupants Dr Waller ordered his servants to pull Hamilton out of his hiding place and hand him over. This was done and he was killed with a pike on the front lawn. Seventeen or eighteen were later charged with murder but they managed to skip the country so no one paid the penalty of death. An interesting element here is that all those who were charged were Ulster Protestants who in those days spearheaded the drive against the British.

Those are the bare bones of the story but the background to it deserves a closer look since it seems to illustrate somewhat eloquently the Irish viewpoint on such happenings. The ordinary people did not see any murder in the killing of Hamilton. In their view he got what he deserved. He was not murdered but he was executed as an active and rather cruel member of a brutal occupying power. This is somewhat easier to understand if we put it in a European setting.

If, for example, during the German occupation of France, the French Resistance killed a pro-German activist in the same way that the Irish killed Hamilton they would be hailed as heroes by the British and American media and more than likely the Establishment of those countries would honour them. But because it happened in British-occupied Ireland it was deemed to be 'murder most foul' and the perpetrators were labelled 'terrorists' and 'criminals'. But the peculiarly Irish element here is that

## INISHOWEN – AILEACH

*the people did not accept this viewpoint.* There are hundreds, if not thousands, of examples of this throughout our history – this divergence of interpretation between the Establishment and the people. The killing of Lord Leitrim is another Donegal example. The men who killed Leitrim were sheltered and protected by the people and after their deaths a memorial was erected in Kindrum to their memory:

> ERECTED TO THE MEMORY
> OF THREE FANAD PATRIOTS
> NEIL SHIELS, MICHAEL HERAGHTY, MICHAEL McELWEE
> WHO BY THEIR HEROISM IN CRATLAGH WOOD
> ON THE MORNING OF APRIL 2nd 1878
> ENDED THE TYRANNY OF LANDLORDISM

This is a rather strange Irish phenomena, and not only did it happen in the past but it is happening today before our very eyes. Military historians deem it to be a basic principle of guerrilla warfare that the guerrillas must have the support of a substantial section of the population, so that they may be housed, fed and protected. Without this help on a large scale they could not continued fighting. Whether we like it or not we have to face the reality that if the IRA in Northern Ireland today did not have this support they would have been defeated long ago. Instead their active campaign has continued uninterrrupted for almost twenty years and shows no sign whatever of diminishing even though bishops and southern Irish politicians have appealed to the public to inform on them. This is a particularly bitter pill which both the Irish and British governments have had to swallow but it has a long tradition behind it – a tradition unlikely to change in the foreseeable future.

There is an old Donegal saying: 'We take our religion from Rome but our politics from Ireland.' Father William

## THE SECRET PLACES OF DONEGAL

MacLaughlin, the parish priest of Cloncha condemned Parnell from the altar and ordered the people not to attend a Parnellite meeting scheduled to take place after Mass. The people ignored him and packed the meeting. Again, during the civil war, the parish priest of Culdaff condemned the IRA but the people ignored him. Later, in 1927, another Culdaff priest read out the names of the Fine Gael candidates in the election as suitable people to vote for but the public ignored him. I cannot help wondering how long it will take the ecclesiastics to realise that they are being ignored by the people precisely because they back the Establishment which on the whole supports injustice. Surely even a nodding acquaintance with the Gospels should put them on their guard.

The Inishowen Peninsula is just one more area of extraordinary beauty in Donegal, teeming with secret places. There is a wonderful tourist route, well signposted, which takes you by way of Malin Head all around the peninsula.

Near Malin Head I went for a short stroll in the fresh summer morning, hoping to make my fortune by searching among the famous Malin Pebbles. The early sunshine fell upon the earth and sea and filled my soul with happiness. Along the shore hundred of thousands of semi-precious stones sparkled and twinkled with a radiance not of this earth: coral, crystal, amethyst, opal, agate and many others, but easy-come riches have always eluded me. Yet there were other even more valuable treasures in this enchanting spot – treasures of nature speaking in many voices through mountains, hills and sea.

Away out into the Atlantic Inishtrahull and Garavan Islands seemed to beckon to me and hold out the same alluring promises that Niamh of the Golden Hair held out to Óisín. In my sailing days I was advised to make an act of perfect contrition if I contemplated sailing through the Garavan Sound with the wind against the tide. It is one of the most dangerous and turbulent stretches of sea on the whole Irish coast and this must surely be caused by the spirits of the deep protecting these enchanting islands. The mystical Inishtrahull Island brings to mind one of the greatest modern Irish poets, D. J. O'Sullivan, who while a lighthouse keeper gave a voice to this lovely island:

> The moon shines on the Isle of Inishtrahull
> Bejewelling nuptial tinting herring-gull,
> May-fly dancing in the balmy air
> And moth returning to its daylight lair.

One of the sad, lonely isolated places of Inishownen is the site of the old monastery at Fahan. I use the word 'sad' because of the deplorable neglect which we have shown towards one of the most historic spots in all Donegal. A lot of the place is covered in briars and nettles. Some are nearly six feet high and may soon obliterate the renowned Cross of St Mura. This was one of the monasteries founded by St Colmcille in the sixth century. St Mura was the first abbot, a member of an extraordinary family who surely deserve an entry in the Guinness book of records in so far as all six brothers were saints! Mura's mortal remains rest under the famous St Mura Cross.

This cross is more in the nature of a headstone than a high cross. Interlaced crosses are carved on each face of the slab and on one face there are two figures and if you look closely you may be able to discern faint inscriptions woven into the dress patterns. Note the inscription in Greek on the northern edge of the slab. Translated this reads: 'Glory and honour to the father, the son and the holy spirit.' The graveyard holds the remains of Agnes Jones, one of Flor-

# THE SECRET PLACES OF DONEGAL

*Slab at Fahan*

ence Nightingale's nurses in Crimea and the neglect of this grave is particularly disgraceful. Because of this all-round neglect here the staggering reality of death and its aftermath again strikes one very forcibly. When somebody who is loved dies those who remain tend the grave for a few years but as time goes on and others die this becomes less and less frequent. And then a day may come when nobody bothers anymore. Nature takes over and slowly obliterates all trace. This is the savage law of life, the universal law, to be born, to live, to suffer, to die, and to be forgotten. And nowhere is it more real than here in Fahan.

Northwards from Fahan there is another grave which brings back memories of a very different kind. It is in the old churchyard at Binnon, in the Clonmany area, and it is the grave of a colonel in the British army named McNeill. He was also one of the worst types of landlord that ever plagued Donegal in the eighteenth century.

Like Lord Leitrim, McNeill's reproductive machinery was somewhat demanding. He, however, specialised in rape and sadism. He travelled around his territory, particularly to fairs, with a guard of four or five British soldiers and they forcibly abducted any of his tenants' daughters that took his fancy. The young girl was then stripped naked and raped by McNeill. When he had his fill any of the soldiers could then have her if the mood was on him.

Once a young girl made her escape by running into a river which was in flood. McNeill and his henchmen waited on the bank, jeering and making obscene remarks until the flood swept the young girl to her death. On another occasion a sixteen-year-old girl, who was dying of consumption managed to escape his clutches. Some months later she died but McNeill did not forget. As the funeral made its way to the graveyard it was stopped by McNeill and his men, who burst open the child's coffin and in front of the heartbroken parents, plunged their swords several times into the corpse. And for those poor people there was no legal redress. McNeill was a British colonel and could do virtually what he liked. But there was of course an 'illegal' one – the kind of one the Irish were forced to use over and over again. A group of Donegal men lay in wait for him and knocked him unconscious with a blow from a heavy stone on the head. One of them, Owen McCole, then castrated McNeill with a billhook. McNeill died some months later, not as a result of the castration but as a result of the wound in his head from the stone. A local explained to me how this happened. 'McCole was a cow doctor,' he said, 'that is a kind of country vet. In them days the cow doctor was mainly occupied in castrating young bulls, so me man was an expert at his job and knew exactly where to cut and sew seeing as there isn't much difference in a bull's landscape down there and a man's. Anyway the good result was that there was one less dangerous doodlebug in Donegal. In a way 'tis a pity he died. 'Twould be great to be able to see him at a fair, with all the lovely lookin' girls around and him not able to do a thing.'

Almost everywhere you go in Donegal you find stories or accounts of incidents like that one, which have in them the makings of a fine novel or a gripping play. Nearby in Clonmany Father Peadar McLoughlin was parish priest and at the same time his brother Donal was Protestant rector. As young students they were travelling to the Irish College in Salamanca when they were shipwrecked off the English coast. They were befriended by a Protestant gentleman and Donal remained with him and became a Protestant while Peadar continued his journey overland to Spain. They both ended up as clergymen on the opposite sides of the fence in Clonmany. Their old mother was heartbroken and time and time again she pleaded with Donal, the Protestant, to come back to the faith of his fathers. She composed the haunting lament:

> Fill, fill, a rún ó,
> Fill, fill, a rún ó, is ná imithigh uaim;
> Fill ort a chuid de'n tsaoghal mhór
> No char fheiceann tú'n ghlóir mur bfilleodh tú.
>
> Come back, come back my love,
> Come back, and do not leave me.
> Come back, my part of life
> If you do not you will never reach glory.

Time and again she even interrupted his sermons in the Protestant church. In the end he put a stop to it by dressing up as Satan and chasing her out of the church grounds. 'Tis said locally that when he died there was a strange gentleman at his funeral dressed very like the man he was impersonating. It is also said that despite the zeal of the mother, Peadar was not over anxious to convert his brother, since to have a close relative in the enemy camp was a distinct advantage. 'Be ye as wise as serpents, but as simple as doves.'

Near the village of Clonmany there lived a tailor by the name of Charles McGlinchy who died in 1954 at the age of ninety-three. The local schoolmaster, Patrick Kavanagh, visited Charles regularly over a period of years and wrote down his story. This wonderful story, sensitively edited by Brian Friel, was published in 1984 under the title *The Last of the Name* and it is without doubt a classic. It ranks with such great Irish books as *The Tailor and Ansty*, *Malachy Horan Remembers*, *The Farm by Lough Gur*, *The Islandman* and *The Man from Cape Clear*. It gives a most marvellous insight into how the people of Donegal lived for the most part of the nineteenth century and it is told with great clarity and rollicking good humour. The poet Seamus Heaney describes it as 'a book full of emotional truth and the beauty of immediate trusting speech, over-brimming with folklore of great imaginative riches.'

If you are in the Clonmany area and you wish to 'make your soul', as the Donegal folk put it, then there is no better place to go than to Glenview or to Butler's Glen where there are magnificent waterfalls. Here in these secret places you can sit, rest and contemplate in the most beautiful surroundings listening to the melodious sound of the dancing water as it leaps and bounds over the dark rocks into the swirling frothy pools – here you can cast away the 'slings and arrows of outrageous fortune' and become a child again:

> Where the pools are bright and deep
> Where the grey trout lies asleep
> Up the river and over the lea
> That's the place for Billy and me.

To the east of Clonmany on Maghermore hill there is a magnificent dolmen with an enormous capstone. Nobody knows what these megalithic monuments really were. Some experts say they were burial places but there is very little evidence for this theory. Unfortunately when many of these experts do not understand something they say it was a grave. Could these megalithic monuments have been an Irish version of energy generators? Could they have been places of spiritual healing? Of meditation? Of prayer? Could they be the remains of great monuments to the lost knowledge, culture and spirituality of the Irish race? The distinguished philosopher Rudolf Steiner wrote:

## INISHOWEN – AILEACH

The inner qualities of the Sun factor, how these permeate the earth and how they are again radiated back from the earth into cosmic space – this was what the druid priest was able to see in the dolmens. The physical nature of the light of the sun was warded off, a dark space was created by the stones, which were set in the soil, with a roof stone above them and in this dark shadowed space it was possible by seeing through the rocks the spiritual nature and being of the sunlight.

There is, however, one thing we can be sure of and that is how little we know of these things and how inadequate are the explanations offered to us by those to whom we turn for enlightenment.

Many people wonder how the large capstones, such as at Magheramore, were put into place. The method was very simple. The standing stones were set into position first. Then they were covered with earth which was gently sloped away for a distance of thirty or forty yards. Timber rollers were put at intervals in this slope and the capstone hauled manually into position. Then the earth was cleared away and just the dolmen remained.

East of Clonmany is Carndonagh, probably the most famous of all Donegal ecclesiastical sites. Here on the roadside is the famous St Patrick's Cross which is probably the oldest high cross in Ireland, dating to the sixth century. These high crosses present us with a mystery almost as great as the dolmens. In my book *The Secret Places of the Burren* I gave my views on these high crosses and I hope I will be pardoned for repeating them here. An immense amount of waffle has been written about the purpose of these high crosses. The truth is that nobody knows what their precise function was. One theory holds that they were merely decorative monuments to the ego-mania of worldly clerics. Another theory is that because of the illiteracy of the people they were used to instruct them in the gospels

*South Pillar, Carndonagh*

at sermon time on Sundays.

High crosses became popular in many parts of Europe as a form of devotion to the True Cross which was supposed to have been found earlier near Jerusalem. Later this was celebrated by the introduction into the liturgy of the Feast of the Exhaltation of the Holy Cross. This distinct oriental flavour can be seen on many of the Irish high crosses. The caps, for instance, have Armenian features. Did the eastern stone-cutters come to Ireland or did our stone-cutters go there? It seems that we had contact very early on with the orient. There is an account in the *Táin* of Cuchulain 'travelling as far as the mountains of Armenia' and much later we read that one of the founders of Rahan and Killeigh monasteries was Cerrui from Armenia. How this oriental influence came about is really unknown. Another unanswered question is why the high crosses passed the main countries of Europe by. They seem to have taken root only in Ireland, Scotland and parts of England as well as in Armenia and Georgia.

If we relate the early Irish litanies and prayers to the scenes on the crosses we find that in many cases the scenes invoked in the prayers are those depicted on the crosses. This could suggest that the prayers were recited in public in front of the crosses or that, as well, individual monks or nuns strolling around the monastery gardens might contemplate the scenes as they prayed. Again there is no certainty. The only thing we can be certain of is that we do not know the answers.

Carndonagh was once a great monastic site. It abounds in relics of the past. But I find it hard to pray or contemplate there. The cars and lorries flying up and down the main road distract me. This is not the fault of Carndonagh, of course, but mine. If I were properly recollected I should be immune from all noise.

Nevertheless one does not have too far to go in search of quiet places. Just outside Malin town there is a small stone structure called the Friar's Cell. Its origins are unknown but during the Penal days it was a hiding place for priests on the run from the British. How many of them spent long anxious days there baptising children, marrying young couples and generally ministering to the needs of the poor hunted Irish while look-out men guarded all the approaches? Despite the primitive nature of the structure it exudes an atmosphere of peace and tranquillity. These little buildings, so neglected now, are our national shrines. The men who hid there and kept alive our faith and culture surely deserve better from us.

Yet I often think that our religion was a far, far greater thing in the Penal days than it is today. Does persecution help? It seems so. There is at present a major vocation crisis in all countries in the free world. There has been a massive decline in those studying for the priesthood; convents and monasteries are closing down and it may well be that soon some of the great orders may cease to exist. But the opposite is the case in the countries behind the Iron Curtain where there has been a massive increase in vocations and where the religious orders and seminaries are unable to accommodate all who seek admission. What is the lesson to be learned from this? Do we thrive in adversity?

Another delightful part of this area are the sand dunes of Lagg. Here you can hide yourself and get lost to the world while you get to know the myriad groups of insects which are all over the place. Do not try to kill them – they have just as good a right to life as you, and after all it is you who have invaded their privacy. If you have a magnifying glass study them and you will be rewarded by seeing bodily structures far more ingenious than the human body – and indeed far more beautiful.

Here too in Lagg you may find some of the most exquisite sea-shells in the world – shells of such gorgeous beauty and intricate artistry that you will find it impossible to say in your heart 'there is no God'. A simple sea-shell can speak volumes to us. Apart from its elfish fairy-like design which is beyond the capabilities of a human artist, it once belonged to someone – some creature of the sea whose life of adventure and drama surpassed that of us humans. And when it died it left behind its indestructible gift of beauty for our enjoyment.

To the east is the village of Culdaff which at one time was a great monastic centre. All that now remains are two unfinished high crosses and a few dismal cells hewn out of solid rock and reputed to be punishment cells for misbehaving monks. In those far-off days the penances were severe for such heinous offences as not saying prayers before meals, coughing in church, dirty finger nails, forgetting to shave, having a thickness of breath after a drop of poteen, breaking wind during divine office, or casting a knowing eye after a woman as she passed. A few of these penances have always intrigued me:

## INISHOWEN – AILEACH

A monk on familiar terms with a woman even though he has not cohabited with her nor lustfully embraced her, shall do penance for forty days on bread and water.

If a woman by her magic destroys a child she has conceived she shall do penance on bread and water for six months and shall abstain from wine and meat for two years. If, however, she gives birth to the child she must fast on bread and water for six years.

If a layman has intercourse with his female slave, the slave must be sold and the layman shall not have intercourse with his own wife for an entire year.

It is interesting that a man can buy and sell slaves with impunity but a little flutter with one is anathema.

The old Irish monks had other strange customs. They were fond of genuflecting, a custom imported from the continent, where the great advocate was Jacob Glúnech – James of the Knees – who used to make 200 genuflections in the day and two hundred at night so that it is said his knees became like those of a camel. A monk of Culdaff went one better. He made 200 at Lauds and 100 at Matins and 100 at each of the canonical hours, i.e. 700 per day. After a while his legs became crippled and he had to reluctantly give up.

Plunging into ice-cold water naked was another penance of the old Irish monks. Indeed in some mixed communities men and women did it together but only at night when they could not offend modesty by looking at one another. It is recorded that a monk of Cloncha saw a sexy little bit passing one day and he was so overcome that 'his parts were affected'. He plunged into a frozen lake for penance but it seems as if the ice froze 'his parts' and his colleagues had to pull him out of the water and light a fire under him to thaw him back to normal.

Yet another monk troubled by thoughts of pretty women burned his penis with a red hot poker, while another castrated himself and a third plunged into a swarm of bees who stung him all over so that he was unrecognisable. What a great pity that the old Bundoran priest with the shake in his head who advised me on these delicate matters was not alive at the time. He could have solved all their problems by the simple expedient of building a handball-alley!

These stupid rules were mostly the invention of local cranks. When the church found out about them they put a stop to them. In AD 813 the Council of Chalons condemned them and in AD 829 the Council of Paris ordered that all copies of these rules be burned. I suppose they were no more than part of growing up, part of the evolution of a negative church of chastisement to a positive church of love and mercy which is coming closer and closer day by day. It has surely taken a long time but then two thousand years is but a flash in the evolution of man.

Of all the monastic remains in Inishowen more than half are located in Culdaff-Cloncha area. St Buadan is the patron saint of Culdaff and it seems as if he was a man of many miracles. He once cured, by an ingenious method, a monk whose legs were paralysed and a nun who had been struck dumb. One night when the nun was asleep Buadan carried the monk to her bed and slipped him in alongside her instructing him to start caressing her. Suddenly the nun woke up and felt the man in the bed with her. She was so shocked that she started shouting, praying and calling for help and in this way restored her voice. When the monk heard her shouting he got such a fright that he jumped out of bed and ran as fast as he could in case he would be caught. In this way his paralysis vanished and everybody lived happily ever after!

Buadan often went sailing in a stone boat and did not sink and when he died he was laid to rest in this same stone boat in Culdaff church. His body never decayed and pilgrims used to come from all parts of Donegal to see it. Local tradition held that he came originally from Ballyshannon and if anyone from there happened to be amongst the pilgrims Buadan knew it instinctively and held out his hand from the tomb for a shake. Unfortunately the Danes burned the church and poor Buadan's body with it.

Also buried nearby is James Hamilton who was Rector here in 1823. This reverend gentleman was married three times and had forty children. Local people say that never were words meant to convey so much as the words 'Rest in Peace' on his grave. It was generally agreed that his rest was a well-earned one.

Some distance beyond Culdaff on the Moville road there is a signpost pointing to Cloncha Church. This church was built on a very ancient monastic site, and is one of the real secret places of Donegal – a place of tranquillity where you can almost hear across the centuries the soft melodious monotone of the monks whose mortal remains lie somewhere around in their nameless unmarked graves. Little is known of Cloncha except that it was a small monastic site founded by St Morialagh about whom even less is known.

These smaller monasteries were rather simple affairs with wattle cells, a church, a refectory and a farm. There is evidence to show that some of them housed male and female religious. One old text tells us that these mixed communities 'had no fear of the wind of temptation'. Indeed it is recorded that one saint had as his fellow scholar the daughter of a king, and even though they lived together for many years he did not recognise her face because he so mortified his eyes that he had only seen her feet. I have the greatest admiration for these old Irish saints, but despite my age, I cannot imagine myself living so long with a king's

*Slab at Cloncha*

daughter without at least casting a furtive eye above her ankles.

I can never come to a place like Cloncha without experiencing a tremendous respect for those old Irish monks. Despite their oddities and crazy penances, such as standing up to their necks in icy rivers, or genuflecting several hundred times a day, their lives showed a burning passion for truth and a dedication to goodness. They saw their role in life as one of self-sacrifice and love. They harmed no one and they brought help and comfort to many a broken heart. Here in the beautiful pastoral surroundings of Cloncha something of their psyche lives on. The large high cross in a nearby field, the extraordinary carved slab by the unknown Fergus MacAllan, the carved mallet and chisel near the doorway probably from the grave of a carpenter, the tombstones with sculptured head – all are in some way, however small, an epitaph to these extraordinary men and women. In the peace and silence of this little churchyard it is hard not to be deeply moved.

On the winding road from Culduff to Greencastle there is a little bay at Kinnagoe where two ships of the Spanish Armada foundered. Some years ago the Derry Sub Aqua Club recovered large quantities of warlike items and brought them to the surface. They included siege cannons, field carriages, storming equipment, muskets, helmets, bullet proof vests. The Armada meant business and had they succeeded the history of Ireland could have changed drastically and the lives of millions of Irish people would have been saved.

Further south is the port of Greencastle, where the delightful, eccentric Frederick Harvey, Fourth Earl of Bristol, and Bishop of Derry ministered. Harvey was a very wealthy man who spent his money on worthwhile projects and he was one of the few Englishmen in Ireland who won the confidence of the Irish. He had a residence across the lough in Downhill and he built the Protestant church in Greencastle so that he could see the porch through a telescope from his home. If he didn't see enough of a congregation there on a Sunday morning he wouldn't bother crossing over for divine service.

Just across the lough from Greencastle is one of the saddest sights. It is Magilligan prison. Here so many young Irishmen suffered ill-treatment simply because they loved their country and wanted to set it free. In January 1987 a Committee of Concerned Relatives held an inquiry into conditions in Magilligan prison, and it makes frightening reading. In some ways Magilligan is worse than the notorious Long Kesh. Bobby Sands, himself suffering in the stench of Long Kesh, penned these poignant lines which express the mind of a prisoner in the six countries:

> Oh! whistling winds why do you weep
>    When roaming free you are.
> Oh! is it that your poor heart's broke
>    And scattered off afar?
> Or is it that you bear the cries
>    Of people born unfree
> Who like your way have no control
>    Or sovereign destiny?
>
> Oh! lonely winds that walk the night
>    To haunt the sinner's soul
> Pray pity me, a wretched lad
>    Who never will grow old.
> Pray pity those who lie in pain
>    The bondsman and the slave,
> And whisper sweet the breath of God
>    Upon my humble grave.

## INISHOWEN – AILEACH

Maybe in a future age in a united Ireland these repulsive places will be turned into national shrines commemorating all those who suffered there. In such an event some dignitary will no doubt be found to perform the opening ceremony.

If you felt inspired to meditate on death in a more light-hearted way there is no better place to do this than at Cooley just north of Moville. Here are the remains of another ecclesiastical site which contain a small stone-roofed building known as The Skull House. All kinds of explanations have been given as to what this house was: an oratory, a saint's grave, a mortuary etc? But the most interesting explanation was given to me by an intelligent local over a few pints. As the refreshments loosened our tongues he gave me his version.

'Hundreds of years ago,' he explained, 'the Donegal tribes were fighting each other nearly every second week and they used to cut the heads off those they killed and stick them up on bushes as a warning to their enemies and also as scarecrows in their gardens to frighten away the birds. Well there was this Christian Brother from Cooley and he didn't rightly fancy this kind of carry on so he sent word for his brother-in-law who was a stone-mason above near Malin in Crockglacknakinnoge and who was a near relation of the Gobán Saor, to call down to Cooley and to build this little stone house in the graveyard for the skulls. So whenever the brother found a head, or half a head or a skull on a bush he gathered it into a little bag he used to carry round with him and brought it home and put it into the wee stone house out of the wind and the rain and the frost. Well the brother died, the Lord have mercy on his soul, and the house was full of skulls and the Abbot of the Christian Brothers was in one hell of a pickle as to what to do with them. Well one fine day there was this tinker who was cleanin' out the monastery privies and the Abbot gave him a fiver to take the skulls away and bury them in some quiet spot where no one would see them. But before he buried them the tinker, who was a bit of a rogue, took all the teeth out of them and made them into false teeth with a bit of solder and lime and turned an honest pound or two by renting out the false teeth for weddings and funerals. In fairness, he washed them first. Anyway the people stopped killing one another and there was no more skulls.'

But should it be a fine sunny day and you are not in the mood for meditating on death then you can enjoy yourself to your heart's content by putting your hand through the hole in the high cross just outside the graveyard. For centuries young couples came here and joined hands through this hole and promised everlasting love and fidelity to each other. So if you are on your own imagine the man or woman of your dreams on the other side of the cross. Hold hands through the hole and maybe you'll get a vision of the true love that is awaiting you. And even if you are an old married couple do it anyway. Maybe your luck would be in and maybe you'd experience that wonderful thrill of old age which John B. Keane calls 'the heat before death'.

All the same Cooley is a very secret place, a very holy place, a place of prayer, but what harm will it do to throw in a little romance, for prayer and love are all the one.

Well, we have slipped along to the end of our little ramble through Donegal and where better to bring it to a close than Aileach, at the southern end of the Inishowen peninsula, which is one of Ireland's most sacred places. It stands strong and clear on a hill nearly a thousand feet high in a most strategic position commanding a superb view over vast tracts of land, lake and sea. All guide books describe

## INISHOWEN – AILEACH

it very well but what do we really know about it? The truthful answer to that question is that we know virtually nothing, except that it is close on 5,000 years old. Most of what has been written about it is pure conjecture.

We do know that the ancient Irish, like so many other ancient civilisations, were great worshippers of the sun which they saw as a supreme being providing them with light, heat and energy. Could it be possible that Aileach was a cathedral of the sun? A place of worship? A venue of retreat? A centre of spiritual and physical energy? We do not know, but in the present state of our knowledge it is a possible explanation.

There is some evidence to show that in the third, fourth and fifth centuries it was the residence of the kings of Ulster. If this is so then there is a strong case for large-scale excavation. A royal palace would have a large number of appurtenances around it: housing for cooks, maids, gardeners, cowhands, butchers, tailors, shoemakers, blacksmiths, clerks, soldiers and all kinds of servants and attendants to look after every need of royal body and mind. It must have been an extensive and a fair-sized town as big as nearby Letterkenny. It is hard to imagine that all these ancillary buildings have vanished without trace. When Ballintubber Abbey was being restored the excavators found an entire monastery underneath the ground. The same happened with Viking Dublin. What would be found if the area surrounding Aileach was excavated and restored? Think of the tourist potential involved. I do not think I exaggerate when I say it could attract hundreds of thousands of visitors every year. But a project like that requires great vision and vision is a commodity which is very scarce among our rulers.

There is a local legend which says that thousands of warriors lie sleeping underneath Aileach awaiting a great Irish leader to awake them and unite the whole of Ireland. Ethna Carbery knew of this legend when she wrote of the north wind:

> Then blow, wind! and snow, wind!
> What matters storm to me,
> Now I know the fairy sleep must break
> And let the sleepers free.

At the beginning of this book I mentioned how different places in Donegal inspired different moods and emotions and Aileach is one such place. As I lay here in the glorious heather the mood that overwhelmed me, I am sad to say, was one of anger and fury as I looked across the border at that part of my country occupied by the British. These occupied six counties are now the last police state in western Europe, where more than forty per cent of the people are brutalised, and at times murdered by a modern-day version of the Gestapo. And all the while Dublin politicians with a prudent eye on their salaries, pensions, perks and privileges collaborate fully with that security force and spend £500,000,000 each year of your money and mine to protect this statelet. Day after day we cringe, genuflect and fawn before the representatives of this occupying power, so that we have now reached the point where we must be the world's greatest arse-lickers – far greater than any third-world country.

Will we always be so or will we ever get off our knees? The first reaction to that question is one of despair. Yet I remember my parents telling me that after the 1916 Rising ninety-five per cent of the Irish people condemned it – every newspaper, every bishop, every public body. Yet within a few years all that had changed and the nation went on to clear out the invader. Will young Irishmen have to occupy

## INISHOWEN – AILEACH

the GPO again and march the lonely corridors of prison to their deaths to arouse us? I hope there is an easier way.

When Yeats was in despair at the low morale of the Irish people he wrote: 'Romantic Ireland's dead and gone and with O'Leary in the grave.' A young American poet, Joyce Kilmer, answered him in a poem which is a fittng end to this book.

> 'Romantic Ireland's dead and gone,
>    It's with O'Leary in the grave,'
> Then Yeats, what gave that Easter dawn
>    A hue so radiantly brave?
>
> Romantic Ireland never dies!
>    O'Leary lies in fertile ground
> And songs and spears throughout the years
>    Rise up where patriot graves are found.
>
> The soil of Ireland throbs and glows
>    With life that knows the hour is here
> To strive again like Irishmen.
>    For that which Irishmen hold dear.
>
> Lord Edward leaves his resting place
>    And Sarsfield's face is glad and fierce.
> See Emmet leap from troubled sleep
>    To grasp the hand of Pádraig Pearse.
>
> There is no rope can strangle song
>    And not for long death takes his toll.
> No prison bars can dim the stars
>    Nor quicklime eat the living soul.

This little poem is, I am afraid, far beyond the understanding of our present day politicians or of the yuppies who aspire to rule us. It would be difficult for an ideal of any kind to penetrate their obtuseness – indeed many of them would find difficulty in spelling the word. But it will undoubtedly strike a chord among the young people of Ireland. They will understand how a young man like Joyce Kilmer could write it and could later give his life for such an ideal. He too fell under a hail of bullets.

All this apart, however, I hope you have enjoyed this little book and that you will bear with my anger, my facetiousness and my philosophising about death. If you have enjoyed it and if it has brought you a few hours happiness in a very confused world, then I will be more than satisfied.

# A READING LIST

The guide to Donegal which I found most helpful was *Donegal – An Exploration* by J. J. Tohill. Other good guides are *A Visitors Guide to Donegal, Leitrim and Sligo* published by Donegal, Leitrim, Sligo Tourism and *The Donegal Guide* published by Bord Fáilte. Apart from those books I mentioned in the text I could recommend the following: *Rambles round Donegal* by Patrick Campbell (Mercier), *The Third Lord Leitrim* by Liam Dolan, *Glencolumbkille* by Aidan Manning, *Autobiography* by Father McDyer (Brandon), *The Great O'Neill* by Seán Ó Faolain (Mercier), *Land War and Eviction in Derryveagh* by Liam Dolan (Annaverna Press), *History of Glenveagh* (National Parks and Monuments Service), *Sin, Sheep and Scotsmen* by W. E. Vaughan (Appletree), *Doe Castle* by Kevin Ward, *Our Inis Eoghain Heritage* by Brian Bonner (Salesian Press), a small pamphlet *Mass Rocks of Innishowen* by Father John Fitzgerald, *Magilligan – A Cause for Concern* and finally that excellent publication *Archaeological Survey of Donegal* edited by Brian Lacy (Donegal County Council).

*MORE INTERESTING TITLES*

# Tomorrow To Be Brave
## John M. Feehan

This is the story of a remarkable and wonderful woman who knew she was going to die a lingering and painful death but who faced up to it with unbelievable courage and who turned her last terrible years on this earth into the greatest years of her life – years of kindness, patience, understanding and unselfishness.

The book starts with her death. We share the anguish of her husband, the author John M. Feehan, lonely, bewildered, angrily rebelling against the unthinkable blow that – like all of us in such situations – he could never believe would really fall. He tells of their early days together; how they weathered the usual joys and sorrows of young married people; how in middle age they began to cast their eyes forward to the time they would enjoy growing old together – and how one day they found out that there was, after all, to be no tomorrow for them. Mary had cancer. She had four years to live. Her husband tells in sober detail of those last four years together when every moment was heightened by the knowledge that their happiness was built of months, then of weeks, and at last only of days and hours. He succeeds in penetrating her inner life, and explains what made her so noble, so cheerful, so unselfish – and indeed so happy – while she was knowingly living under the shadow of death.

# The Wind that Round the Fastnet Sweeps

## John M. Feehan

There are moments in the life of every human being when he becomes haunted with the longing to leave behind the turmoil and tension of daily living, to get away from it all and to escape to a clime where true peace can be found. There are many practical reasons why most of us cannot do this so the next best thing is to read the story of one who tried.

John M. Feehan sailed, all by himself, in a small boat around the coast of West Cork in search for this Land of the Heart's Desire, this Isle of the Blest.

. . . brilliant. . . the Irish story of San Michele.' – John B. Keane.

# The Magic of the Kerry Coast
## John M. Feehan

This is a sequel to the best-selling *The Wind that Round the Fastnet Sweeps.* In it John M. Feehan continues his odyssey from Crookhaven up the coast of Kerry to the Skellig Rocks and the Blasket Islands. It follows the same pattern – a little sailing, a little thinking, a little laughing, a little drinking and once again we meet a marvellous collection of those strange and unusual characters who always seem to run across the author's path and which he describes with such understanding and humanity.

# The Magic of the Shannon
## John M. Feehan

Following the success of *The Wind that Round the Fastnet Sweeps* and *The Magic of the Kerry Coast* John M. Feehan gives us another travel book of memorable beauty.

This time he cruised two hundred miles of the River Shannon, from Killaloe to Lough Key, calling at all the little country harbours on the way. Again we meet a variety of strange and unusual characters: a tramp of the old school, a theologically-minded pickpocket, a literary courtesan, a bizarre corpse-washer with an eye for the artistic, a specialist in the romantic moods of frogs, snails and hedgehogs. These and many others, people the pages of *The Magic of the Shannon*. With a sensitive and rare touch he describes those precious moments of time when earth and sky and water are blended into flashes of unforgettable loveliness. He sees the pain and the sorrow of human suffering as well as the rollicking laughter of human joy. Dominating all is the majestic Shannon with a thousand years of history around every bend.

# The Secret Places of the Burren
## John M. Feehan

Following the success of *The Magic of the Kerry Coast, The Magic of the Shannon* and *The Wind That Round the Fastnet Sweeps* John M. Feehan gives us another travel book of memorable beauty.

This time he searches out the hidden corners of the Burren, those secluded places where time stands still and where nature speaks its secret language to the human spirit.

Although at times controversial, cutting through sham and pretence wherever he meets it, he writes with great charm, skill and sympathy, and with a deep love of the countryside and its people.

He sees the mystery, the beauty and the sense of wonder in ordinary things and brings each situation to life so that the reader feels almost physically present.

This is a most delightful Irish travel book that can be read again and again.

www.ingramcontent.com/pod-product-compliance
Ingram Content Group UK Ltd.
Pitfield, Milton Keynes, MK11 3LW, UK
UKHW041414180426
11947UKWH00007B/127